PENG

LILY ON 1

Nancy Keesing was born in Sydney in 1923 and was educated at Sydney Church of England Girls' Grammar School, Frensham and Sydney University. During the war she worked as a clerk in the Department of the Navy, and after the war she was employed as a social worker at the Royal Alexandra Hospital for Children. She has been a committee member and also vice-president of the English Association of New South Wales; a member of the Management Committee of the Australian Society of Authors and editor of the Society's journal, the *Australian Author*, and a member, and later chairman, of the Literature Board of the Australia Council. She is involved with the NSW National Book Council and other writers' organizations, and is also active in educational affairs. In 1979 Nancy Keesing was made a member of the Order of Australia.

Victoria Roberts was born in New York in 1957 and grew up in Mexico and Australia. Her piquant cartoons have graced the pages of the *Sydney Morning Herald*, *Cleo*, the *Age* and other publications. She has illustrated a number of children's books and had several exhibitions of her 'serious' work. She has also illustrated her own calendar, *Transports* and Michele Field's *Oz Shrink Lit*. Her secret ambition is to be as famous as Picasso and as rich as Getty.

Nancy Keesing

Lily on the Dustbin

Slang of Australian Women and Families

Drawings by Victoria Roberts

PENGUIN BOOKS

Penguin Books Australia Ltd,
487 Maroondah Highway, P.O. Box 257
Ringwood, Victoria, 3134, Australia
Penguin Books Ltd,
Harmondsworth, Middlesex, England
Penguin Books,
40 West 23rd Street, New York, N.Y. 10010, U.S.A.
Penguin Books Canada Ltd,
2801 John Street, Markham, Ontario, Canada
Penguin Books (N.Z.) Ltd,
182-190 Wairau Road, Auckland 10, New Zealand

First published by Penguin Books Australia, 1982
Reprinted 1982, 1983, 1985

Copyright © Nancy Keesing, 1982

Typeset in Concorde Light by
Dovatype, Melbourne

Made and printed in Australia by
The Dominion Press–Hedges & Bell

CIP

Keesing, Nancy, 1923–
Lily on the dustbin.

ISBN 0 14 006634 9.

1. English language – Australia. I. Roberts,
Victoria. II. Title.

427'994

To the Australian Folk

Contents

Acknowledgements

The help of many people is acknowledged in the text. I do thank Reta Grace for her careful typing. Otherwise, without the response of countless Australian people this book could not have been compiled. I have dedicated it accordingly.

Introduction

A GOOD ROOT IN MY DRAWERS

The lily on the dustbin

He's tight as a mouse's ear

She's tight as a mouse's ear

MY STOVE COOKS SLOW AS A

WET WASHDAY

This book has been compiled with the help of several hundred living Australians of all ages, from people in their nineties to young children. Nearly all the words and phrases in it are used by them today: some are recently coined, others perpetuate the speech of countless Australian women and their families since the early nineteenth century. A few expressions have been abandoned because slang can cancel slang; women who once got out brooms and buckets to have 'a good root round the house' or 'a good root in my drawers' today adopt a less equivocal term for a thorough cleaning of rooms.

Australian women, men and children responded to my appeals for women's and domestic slang with joyful generosity. Hundreds wrote letters containing lists of examples, each carefully explained. Others joined radio 'phone-in' sessions so enthusiastically that at one radio station I took calls to the switchboard for nearly one hour after the on-air session was over.

'The lily on the dustbin' (or perhaps garbage tin, or dirt bin) was one phrase that early became, for me, a symbol of a whole range of women's speech and domestic language that I call

'Sheilaspeak' and 'Familyspeak', and that has had an inexplicably small place in standard compilations of Australian slang and colloquialisms. The lily means different things to different people and sometimes several things to one person. Those who use it are most often women, but their sons and grandsons remember their words. Where the lily originally grew I know not, neither do I care. Much Australian slang has been imported, though it is adapted to our own speech needs. Consider the lily: sometimes it expresses incongruity, and some women liken an over-dressed person to the lily. But most often it means a person left languishing. Sheilaspeak and Familyspeak, too, have languished, forlornly disregarded by philologists and linguists.

Sidney J. Baker, who remains one of the greatest authorities on Australian slang, is an exception. In *The Australian Language* (1966 edition), he included a fair range of domestic speech, and he was very much aware of its existence. He, like me, relied a great deal on his ears. Later collectors have preferred to use chiefly novels, Hansard, newspapers and other kinds of publications. These are excellent sources but inevitably limited. Reliance on print may be one of the factors that cause a detectable male bias in many collections. I do not think this bias is deliberate, although it is certainly noticeable. For instance, most linguists comment on Australians' national penchant for abbreviating words, most often with the suffix 'ie' — bickie for biscuit and so forth. Sometimes, with the same suffix, words are enlarged so that a can, or tin of beer becomes a 'tinnie'. Slang collections offer lists of this practice, but only Baker, I think, listed 'lippie' for lipstick; and even he overlooked many others with feminine or domestic connotations, like 'pinnie', 'chimmie' and 'cardie'.

Widespread expressions used solely or chiefly by women have been overlooked completely: 'to spend a penny' for instance. Some words are collected in the masculine senses of their slang and overlooked in their feminine usage: one of these is the word 'scrape'. Its use as both noun and verb, usually by men, to mean copulation has been recorded, but its widespread

4

use by women as a slang synonym for a curette or an abortion has not. *'He's* tight as a mouse's ear' said of a man means he's mean. *'She's* tight as a mouse's ear' signifies something entirely different.

Although deliberate sexual discrimination may not be responsible for omissions of this order I am convinced sexist-seeming blind spots have occurred because of over-reliance on print. G. A. Wilkes's excellent *A Dictionary of Australian Colloquialisms* (Sydney University Press, 1978) is an invaluable recent reference book; another useful one is Bill Hornadge's *The Australian Slanguage* (Cassell Australia, 1980). Wilkes, whose work is scholarly, but also popular and entertaining, confined his examples to what has surfaced in printed sources. Hornadge uses chiefly the printed sources mentioned previously but gives examples from direct speech.

In fairness to both Wilkes and Hornadge it is necessary to note that, recent as their books are, they were completed before several significant novels by young women were published; among these are *Puberty Blues* by Gabrielle Carey and Kathy Lette (McPhee Gribble, 1979) and *Early Marks* by Barbara Pepworth (Angus & Robertson, 1980). These novels, irrespective of their other good qualities, are notable for their range and frankness of slang as it is used, or has been used, by young Australian women from 1970 onwards. The collections of both Wilkes and Hornadge might have contained fewer gaps had such novels and also recent plays and published works of oral history, been available to them.

Because of developments in the past couple of years in the kinds of books women have published, and because, too, of recent publications emerging from women's studies courses and feminist presses, I was tempted to pillage printed work, also. The response I received from 'the folk' persuaded me not to do so. It was overwhelming and came from people and parts of the country unlikely to be accessible to research assistants and students.

In noting the different kinds of words being used by young novelists and in Sheilaspeak and Familyspeak, however, I perceived a seeming puzzle or paradox. After all, women writers have shaped a major part of Australian literature throughout this century. Wilkes, particularly, has quoted colloquialisms extensively from writers of the calibre of Ernestine Hill, Kylie Tennant and Dorothy Hewett among others. Yet the colloquialisms he selected from such feminine sources were either chiefly in general use, or masculine use.

It would seem, then, that until recently, most Australian women authors who recorded slang preferred those kinds of usages. Naturally, for male characters and speakers that is appropriate, and authors have an unquestionable right to choose whatever topics, themes, backgrounds and characters their art demands. It became increasingly clear, however, that for some reason most Australian novelists — men as well as women — between 1920 and 1970 chose not to write about kids, kitchens and kindergartens or, when they did, chose to select certain colloquial terms and reject a whole range of others.

Fashion, community attitudes and the requirements and expectations of readers must have a good deal to do with the expressions that writers select, whether in the recent past or today. Undoubtedly, one of the consequences of the new feminism and the women's movement since the 1960s is that more and more women are nowadays comfortable to write as women; a compulsion to write as 'one of the boys' has been removed. These observations have nothing to do with the acceptance of women writers as such. I do not think Australian women have been disadvantaged in finding publishers or audiences, though there is some evidence that tertiary institutions have discriminated against women's books when deciding what literature shall be presented to, and studied by, students.

Perhaps the pendulum of reform set swinging by the women's movement has swung too far in another direction. I am now heartily wearied of reading novels, both local and from overseas, that with inordinate length and explicitness describe menstruation, miscarriage induced or otherwise, the less attractive aspects of child care and nurture and teenage sexual activity.

Nevertheless, necessary change and reform are usually

extreme in literature as in politics, religion and education. Elizabethan and Restoration licence and indecency was given beneficial new directions by the puritans, although a few excellent babies, one being drama, were thrown out with that bathwater. Pendulums always swing back, and eventually, inevitable and often desirable exaggerations are abandoned in favour of a more settled balance. This happened after the *Lady Chatterley's Lover* 'pornography' trial. For a few years, countless authors of consequence, including one Nobel Prize winner, introduced hitherto forbidden topics and words to a point of absurdity and satiety. But when a sense of the appropriate returned, the veracity and directness achieved by that interlude of excess remained and adds to the richness of writing now.

There is another disadvantage when printed sources are relied on too heavily: they are the tip of an iceberg only. Newer community usages may be quite widespread before a novelist hears them; after that only those that best suit the theme, characters or mood will be selected. Books never use fully the vocabulary, either formal or colloquial, of any writer. A politician, journalist, radio speaker or sporting commentator says what is most forceful or funny at the moment.

By contrast the Australians who have helped me tell me what they say now, and when and why, and also what their grandparents, relatives and neighbours say and said. Many of them explain precisely how certain colloquialisms have fared over several generations of a family, and in their turn they pass their own colloquialisms to their children and grandchildren. They also record what their children are saying and inventing now. One young father gave a splendid illustration of how new usages emerge, allowing me to 'get in on the ground floor' of some lasting slang:

You might like to hear of my younger daughter's contribution to philology. When she was about six she 'invented' the verb 'to greedy'. For example, 'Mummy, Jamie's greedied my lollies!' Over the last five years *this usage has pervaded the whole family, including aunts, uncles and cousins*, [my italics, N.K.] so that now one might hear 'Hey, don't

7

you greedy all those nails, I'll be needing them.' I think 'greedy' is much more expressive than 'take', 'pinch' or 'steal', don't you?

Since I began this project I have spoken to numerous women who say they neither know nor use slang. Then one complains her old stove cooks 'as slow as a wet washday' and soon members of a group contribute words that they suddenly realise they use or hear frequently. In a gossipy group of women friends one item of gynaecological or scandalous import injected into a conversation can introduce an essentially feminine range of slang, euphemisms and colloquial phrases and, also, an altered tone of voice.

In assembling this collection I have had to make choices and decisions about close variants, but I have not censored anything, though a few expressions are impolite, and a few sound cruel, especially out of context. Admittedly, some letters contained terms like 'I'm writing because I couldn't tell you this on the radio' or 'you won't be able to use this, it's rude' or 'rather vulgar'; but these apologies were for harmless women's swear words, or mildly impolite words like 'pee' and 'bum'. As far as I could gather from handwriting, generational differences were detectable; older people apologised for usages, even nursery words, that younger ones recorded without qualification. Older women were reticent about synonyms for menstruation though several of them remarked that 'things like this are much more talked about now'. Menstruation was one area of speech where I had to be selective. I suspect there are as many synonyms for it and its appurtenances as there are girls' schools in Australia, and, as with much school-age slang, many terms are ephemeral. I have included widespread usages only.

There have been groups of people in this country since 1788 whose chief language is not English. And Aboriginal languages supplied many early Australian names for flora, fauna, places and other things. The chapter called 'Half English — half something else' gives a small sample of Australian domestic slang derived from non-English languages. I hope someone better qualified than I am may soon provide more examples of these aspects of multi-cultural speech.

In many parts of Australia, Aboriginal languages are still spoken, and urban Aborigines have an extensive range of colloquial speech incorporating their own and English words. Glossaries of these words and phrases are available. (A comprehensive one for Perth is included in Archie Weller's fine novel *The Day of the Dog*, published by Allen & Unwin in 1980.) I regret that several requests I made for first-hand information about Aboriginal usages were unsuccessful, and because of my 'no printed sources' policy I have not re-printed examples from published books or lists.

I decided not to include certain specialised categories of colloquial speech, such as the slang of sub-groups like surfies, bikies, the drug culture and the jargon of the business and commercial worlds because, apart from being ephemeral, these 'slanguages' seldom contain words only or chiefly used by women or in family settings. The lore, language and games of schoolchildren is a field well researched in Australia and published in *Cinderella Dressed in Yella* (Turner, Factor and Lowenstein, Heinemann Education Australia, 1978); I chose, therefore, not to stray over-much into that area.

Of the several hundred people who contributed to this book some indicated I might use their name, others asked me not to, most did not express their wishes. I have no idea of the identities of those who responded to radio phone-ins or of the few letter writers who gave neither signature nor address. Consequently, it seemed best and fairest not to include the names of informants as a general rule that I only varied when information came from fellow writers or when historical value made a positive attribution desirable.

I acknowledge many kinds of help elsewhere, but my chief gratitude is to the Australian 'folk' who invented this speech and keep it alive and constantly renewed. I hope they will enjoy what I have made of their material as much as I enjoyed the making. My effective cut-off date was 31 August 1981, and to those people whose letters arrived after that I apologise for having to leave out some interesting material. If/when this book is re-issued I shall include extra examples and I shall look forward to hearing from readers who have comments and/or additional Sheilaspeak and Familyspeak.

Eventually, all letters and my notes, research and working materials will be donated to the Australian Language Research Centre at the University of Sydney. 'Waste not, want not' as my granny would have said.

1

How old is a Bondi tram?

LEGS LIKE A MULLINGAR HEIFER

A threepenny lick

Wish in one hand and wee in the other

Full up to Dolly's wax

QFRTB - QUITE FULL READY TO BUST!

'What's in your handbag..'
'Fly-paper for a nosey stickybeak.'

Snug as a bug in a rug

There are many analogies between slang words and phrases and folklore. They are close kin for the important reason that they arise from the folk, who are all of us. It is seldom possible to discover who first invented and used a slang phrase, or to determine why some colourful words and expressions 'catch on' while others remain unique to a family or extended family. Also mysterious is why some colloquial speech goes out of date while other phrases seem immortal. No trams have rattled out to Bondi for decades now, but 'he shot through like a Bondi tram' is still popular Australia-wide: I recently collected it from Western Australia, and in Rockhampton, Queensland, it has become a Bondi bus.

'Snug as a bug in a rug' is immortal and derives, it is usually supposcd, from Banjo Paterson's 'A Bush Christening'. Did Paterson invent the phrase or, as he did with 'Waltzing Matilda', include an already popular folk colloquialism in an even more popular ballad?

Some of the examples I received belonged — I thought — in the family private joke category. Then someone apparently unrelated contributed the same or a similar usage. One correspondent wrote of a person having 'legs like a Mullingar heifer'.

13

Weeks later a woman told me, 'One thing my father often said was "She has a face like a Mullingar heifer". But you won't want that — Mullingar is in Ireland.'*

Many colloquialisms that sounded rare and unusual when I first collected them proved to be widespread. The 'lily on the dustbin' is an example. I had not encountered the lily until my first radio plea for women's slang. A caller gave two terms for a girl left forlornly waiting at an agreed meeting place for a friend who failed to arrive: 'left dying in the hole', or 'left like the lily on the dustbin'. No one else has instanced the first of these expressions, but the lily is in common use and has several meanings. One woman says to look like a lily on a dustbin (or garbage or dirt bin) is to dress inappropriately for an occasion and/or to wear over-fussy, frilly clothes. Another uses it for a variety of incongruous matters: an informal or poor family meal table might have newspaper instead of a cloth and cracked and battered utensils, and one pretty milk jug stands in the centre of it like a lily on a dustbin.

And, finally, there was the story of a woman academic who was born, and spent her early childhood, in a depressed slum area of Sydney in the 1930s. Her mother would not allow her to play with the barefoot and shabby neighbourhood children and took great pains to dress the child well. One day, holding her mother's hand, she emerged from their terrace house in an elaborate dress, white socks, patent-leather shoes and with her hair twisted into long corkscrew ringlets. 'Blime!' exclaimed the man next door. 'Just *look* at the lily on the dustbin!'

Sometimes when slang goes out of date it might *seem* obvious that this is because it refers to outmoded things. But what seems obvious is frequently inexplicable. A small scoop of ice-cream

---

*Later again it seems, the heifer has been naturalised — a Menindie or Mungindie heifer is in currency.

on a cone was a 'penny lick' and a standard size scoop was a 'threepenny lick'. Obviously, these expressions are no longer heard because, for one thing, basic sizes of ice-cream in our inflationary era now cost a great deal more than a penny or threepence, and also because Australia adopted metric currency almost two decades ago. How then does one explain the great number of current colloquialisms that perpetuate stable prices and pre-metric currency? 'As silly as a two bob watch' remains a common synonym for silliness and takes no more account of either inflation or metrication than does 'not the full quid', 'a shilling short' (some say 'a shingle' short), or '19/6 in the pound', which are still used for stupidity or intellectual handicap, also. When one experiences sudden enlightenment 'the penny drops'. The explanation cannot be that older people cling to phrases they have used all their lives while young folk invent or prefer newer ones. The latter continue to use countless out-of-date expressions as well as recent coinages. That

As silly as a two bob watch

specifically feminine usage 'to spend a penny' (men's urinals are free) may well have as long a life as to be 'down in the dumps', which in Australian general slang, derives from the 'dumps' cut from Spanish dollars in 1813; these became legal currency in early Australia.

I am sure that much domestic and feminine slang owes its long life to the manner in which it is passed from one generation to another. Young women at home, and older women caring for small children, are less accessible to new coinages than are teenagers, men who drink in hotel bars and other groups who quickly embrace and then quickly discard new, colourful language. (The slang of teenage 'surfies', for instance, changes rapidly and so does the jargon of the business world and the cult language of drug addiction. Each of these 'slanguages' is rapidly aware of overseas inventions via specialist media, travel and personal contacts.) I can best explain this with examples.

In *The Australian Language* Baker spoke of 'an interesting nursery cant phrase that has developed as a set answer to a child's question "What's that?" — "Flypaper for a stickybeak".' As soon as I publicised my search for family slang my seven-year-old neighbour, Ben, rushed in to tell me his 'favourite new joke'. His grandmother had reprimanded him for fidgeting with her handbag, and he had asked 'Well what *is* in your handbag?' 'Fly-paper for a nosey stickybeak,' Gran snapped. Part of Ben's pleasure in this joke was that he had never seen a fly-paper or heard of a stickybeak. Gran had to explain herself, and Ben found the whole episode deliriously funny.

Small children differ from adults in their attitude to humour. Most adults nearly 'crawl up the wall' if someone not only tells a joke but then explains it. Children, by contrast, adore having jokes explained to them and often infuriate adults when they, in turn, tell a story and insist on elucidating every last, obvious point.

One elderly retired schoolteacher gave an example of how this kind of saying spreads and may change subtly. His grandmother migrated from Scotland to Australia at the turn of the century. When he was a small boy and said 'I wish I could have another piece of cake', she would reply, 'You can wish in one hand and wee in the other and ye ken which ane will be fu' fust.' During forty years of teaching in New South Wales schools he often made this rejoinder to his pupils but altered 'wee' to 'spit' and, presumably, used a local accent.

When my children were small a man, then in his eighties, sat back from our table after lunch and announced, 'I'm full up to dolly's wax!' It had to be explained that dolls once had delicate, modelled wax heads with a neck shaped so that it could be sewn to a stuffed rag body. 'Full up to dolly's wax', therefore, meant the same as 'full up to pussy's bow', 'full to the neckline' or, as their grandmother often said, 'QFRTB' (Quite full, ready to bust!). Dolls have not had wax heads for so long that it seems likely the phrase dates from at least the eighteenth century. I now know this expression is used by many Australian families (as is QFRTB, and its variant FURTB — full up ready to bust). One elderly correspondent told me that her grandmother, who lived at Port Arthur in Tasmania in the 1820s, taught 'dolly's wax' to her mother while she, in turn, has introduced it to her children and grandchildren.

What Iona and Peter Opie called *The Lore and Language of Schoolchildren* (Oxford University Press, 1959), which is an authoritative collection of children's colloquialisms, game chants and rhymes, is just as conservative as domestic lore and language. *Cinderella Dressed in Yella* provides copious evidence that Australian schoolchildren are as conservative as their overseas counterparts. New lore and new words constantly enter this special and well-recorded field, but little of the old vanishes absolutely, though it may alter across generations and from place to place.

2

Remember, a shut mouth catches no flies

HOME DEVIL AND STREET ANGEL

Mystery bags (sausages)

'You're nosey enough to want to know
the ins and outs of a chook's bum.'

A nifty nightie

A MARY PICKFORD IN THREE ACTS

Beating the gun with an APC

Put the lid on! Do you want the whole street to know our business?' rouses an exasperated woman. 'Come on inside.' A door slams, and thereafter only a fly on the wall hears the rest of that dingdong row.

We value our privacy both individually and as families. A Cessnock, New South Wales, mother, seeing her children off to school, warned them not to recount private family business to their friends with the phrase 'Remember, a shut mouth catches no flies'.

Home is where if it itches you can scratch it, let your hair down, tell home truths: 'She's a home devil and a street angel'.

By the end of the week many a mother is 'strapped for cash' or without 'a brass razoo'. In this plight she often embarks on a policy of Peter and Pauling among her budgetary nest eggs — she robs Peter to pay Paul. She will also economise with food, serving 'mystery bags' (sausages) or some other cheap but substantial fare to her family. Like many a woman before her she may echo Bob the Swagman and remark that, 'if it won't fatten it will fill'. One Bondi battler, during the Depression of the 1930s, would contrive stews and casseroles from all manner of cheap ingredients and put the meal on her table with the

21

flourish 'open the dish and dishcover the riddle!'. A good deal of gallantry underlies much domestic usage.

When the chaos of the breakfast table is cleared away and the dishes 'done' the housewife who is fortunate enough to have all her children 'off her hands' may turn on her 'trannie' to follow her favourite 'talk show'. (These days you won't hear a 'soapie' until later.) Disembodied voices cajole, argue and report a daily tally of disaster and despair while she makes the beds and 'pulls through' her house. 'Nothing keeps as well as housework', but it has to be done — 'what can't be cured must be endured' — or else you'll have rooms 'all over the place like a madwoman's breakfast' and windows festooned with 'Irish curtains' (cobwebs). On a particularly busy day the house has to 'do' with 'a lick and promise'.

If she stubs her toe — and she easily might because she is probably wearing thongs, or jandals if she's a New Zealander or flip-flops if English, or bare feet (Australians 'wear' bare feet*) — her exclamation could be a useful indicator of her age.

Until the mid-twentieth century — during and after World War II — Australian families seldom swore or used coarse or blasphemous expletives at home, and women seldom swore anywhere. These conventions obtained in households of every class in city and country, except for atypical families where someone was violent, drunken or notably foul mouthed. Children were expected to leave schoolyard smutty talk outside with their muddy shoes; their elders instilled and expected reasonable manners and reasonable restraint.

In the work place, drinking in hotel bars, playing or watching sport and most of all in the armed services during two world wars, the Australian male achieved an international reputation for blasphemy and coarse colloquial speech, but he would turn his profane 'slanguage' on and off like a tap — firmly *off* at the doorstep of his home. Familyspeak may be frank, salty and

---

*One correspondent reports a young mother in the 1950s 'who used to "wear" garments on her child: "I won't wear his best clothes on him today".'

often unkind but it is not what Australians of older generations called 'dirty', though some of them apologise for one or two harmless 'rude' expressions.

A woman born at about the turn of the century might have said 'Blast', but unlike many of her daughters and even more of her granddaughters, she would never have said 'Shit!'. She might have said 'shite'*, however which was considered allowable, or 'sugar' which was a widespread substitute. This vanished convention was paradoxical rather than hypocritical. Men who used aggressive expletives among themselves were affronted by a man who did not 'remember himself' or 'guard his tongue' in mixed company. Many drinking men tried to 'remember themselves' when the barmaid was in earshot. Men of these generations were often anxious when they 'landed' in hospital for surgery, fearing what awful expressions might escape their lips in front of women nurses when the men were emerging from anaesthetics. A polite fiction prevailed that women would not know the meaning of many a terrible word even if they did hear it; this was sometimes true. At the time of the *Lady Chatterley's Lover* trial (1960) I knew several older Sydney women who were genuinely puzzled about what all those frightful four-letter words were.

Women used to let off steam domestically with a fine range of substitute expletives: 'Holy Moses!', 'Holy mackerel!', 'great balls of fire', 'good gravy', 'jumping Jehosophat!' and 'muddy great bucket of pitch!'. Wrote one correspondent, now in her forties,

My mother who wouldn't say damn for sixpence would, when frustrated beyond patience yell on top note: 'You upjumped, downtrodden, uncivilized son of a seacook' and look visibly relieved ... as we got older and more of a handful she learned to swear mildly, but was never comfortable about it.

Another letter says,

My mother was brought up in the strict Protestant tradition: no dancing, no smokes, no booze. If you said 'damn' or 'blast' you were heavily into swearing. However ... if she had to get up very early she talked

---

*THE AYATOLLAH KHOUMEINI IS A SHI—ITE
(1981 graffiti)

about getting up at 'sparrowfart' [and] if you had no claim to great beauty you were 'as ugly as a hatful of arseholes'.

These women, within their own four walls, understood the efficacy of 'shock value'. Unlike dad and his mates, whose conversation if you overheard it clandestinely was a fairly predictable succession of 'bloodies', when mum exploded she did it with conviction.

Some people wrote to say how surprised they were to realise that granny or aunty, whom they always considered to be strict and genteel, if not positively prudish, used words and phrases that are 'rude'. The rude word in question is very often 'bum'. Children themselves understood that 'bum' was a 'rude word', so presumably these incongruous utterances surprised them greatly and seemed particularly funny and memorable: 'What's for lunch?' 'Snake's bum on biscuit.' 'You're nosey enough to want to know the ins and outs of a chook's bum.' An aunt remembered for her puritanical opinions disapproved of girls who whistled. 'You're lucky to have a chook's bum to whistle through', she chided her startled niece. Many people listed 'bottie' as a genteelism, but one gave 'bum' as its synonym implying that 'bottie' was the politer word.

Some women who are careful to keep up appearances and to speak and behave in a seemly fashion in public, and also in the presence of husbands and grown sons, seem to feel considerable relief in saying 'rude' words to small children, including young boys, and in sharing risqué jokes and observations with daughters and other family females.

My father, despite a profession that chiefly took him among men in his working hours, and years of service with the first AIF, was a straightlaced and strangely innocent man who had a sense of fun rather than a sense of humour. He greatly relished puns of a heavy-handed order (his own and other people's) and enjoyed a joke if it was labelled with a capital 'J' and not 'smut'. He wrongly believed, and often complained, that my mother had no sense of humour; she did, but not of a kind she could share with him.

25

The first time I ever realised this was when I was about eight or nine and engrossed in a beautifully illustrated book of children's stories retold from the classics. One tale was about 'Psyche, the loveliest maiden that the people of the country had ever seen'. How then, I puzzled, could she have had such a hideous name?

'But her name is not Pss-itch,' my mother laughed. In further explaining the rules of English spelling and pronunciation of words derived from Greek she said, 'The pee is silent as in surf bathing.' It was the first of countless times we giggled helplessly together, and I recall later how I realised that not only had mum used that wicked word 'pee' and found it funny, but that other people, presumably even my mother, wee-ed in the ocean!

Just as I found out I was not alone in contributing my drop to the Pacific, I have discovered that other women, and several much younger than I, first recognised an essential sisterhood with their mothers and other female relatives when these older people admitted them to this order of joke. A sophisticated journalist remains surprised to recall that her mother often said, 'Every little helps as the old woman said when she pee-ed in the sea.' A woman in her eighties contributed her mother's version: 'Every little helps as the old woman said when she widdled in the well.' A media executive, whose mother never swore, still experiences and conveys a sense of astonishment when recalling that her mother, on such occasions as kicking off a

pair of smart, uncomfortable shoes or relaxing in a loose house-coat on a hot day, would exclaim, 'Ah, that's better, as the old woman said when she removed the french letter that had been there since Armistice Day!'

Each generation in its turn seems surprised to discover that parents, grandparents and forbears to the umpteenth degree were probably very much like ourselves. Sex was not invented yesterday. Neither was physical comfort.

The first time I found myself in North Queensland in summer I wondered how pioneer women bore their long dresses, thick stockings and laced boots in such awful heat. Often, they would have smelled a cane burn somewhere nearby whose thin, per-vasive ash would darken their houses and furnishings by morn-ing. But they would not have had a strong jet of water from a hose to clean the mess away; they would have to sweep and scrub ash, and heavy volcanic soil, and all the detritus of a house, from their floors. No vacuum cleaners, or iced drinks for them. Then on a Monday they would sweat over a wood-fired copper to wash personal and domestic linen for a large family and press it later with a mangle, flat iron or, for the innovative and affluent, a 'Mrs Potts' (a pre-electric heated iron).

'Horses sweat, men perspire and ladies flush' my grand-mother used to say. Presumably pioneer women in the sugar districts 'flushed', at least in 'shimmies' and 'pettis' and bodices and long dresses with a clean 'pinny' over all. (Starched cotton for the well off, a patchwork of flour bags for the rest.)

'Not on your life,' said Jim, as I will call him, who, just then was answering all my eager, ignorant questions. 'So soon as the men and schoolkids were gone from the house they stripped to the basics. A few did their housework in the nuddy.'

It was Jim who had taken me for a drive inland, west of Mackay, and pointed out that here watercourses flowed 'on the wrong side of the sand'. In other words, what looked like a com-pletely dry creek would yield good flowing water a few feet down. I had no reason to question Jim's veracity.

So much for sugar town. About twenty years ago a woman writer published a novel about a mining town in western

Queensland and contrived an amusing (so she thought) incident about a woman who stripped off her clothes to do her
housework. The book gave enormous offence locally and was
angrily denied, at least for older generations — the pioneers. It
was averred that modesty counted above everything for the
white women who first made homes in that harsh district; that
anyone who couldn't care for home and family fully clad was
a 'softy' and had no business there.

I suspect the truth to be that some women did strip and others
would never dream of doing so. Granted that each group was
undoubtedly modest and secretive about private matters, close
neighbours could well remain ignorant of each other's intimate
practices behind closed doors. (No more do I know whether my
suburban neighbours do summertime chores in bra and panties
or less.)

Jokes and slang sometimes lend clues to vanished secrets.
When I was six I recuperated from a tonsillectomy in the house
of my childless and widowed aunt. Also staying with her was
the flighty flapper daughter of a Melbourne friend. This
delicious and beautiful young woman wore scanties, so I heard,
and scent, and worried my aunt no end. 'And,' said my aunt to
my grandmother, 'last week when it was so hot I'm sure she slept
in a nifty nightie.' 'I don't believe it!' said my shocked grandmother. 'And how could you tell?' 'Her sheet looked as if it had
been wet,' said my aunt. 'What's a nifty nightie?' asked I. 'Little
pitchers!'* said my aunt, who had plainly forgotten I was in the
room. What *was* a nifty nightie? Why so shocking?

* 'Little pitchers, or pigs, have long ears.'

28

My friend, the novelist Kay Brown, née Ronan, who lived as a child before World War I in the North West cattle country and Broome, provided an explanation. I had asked Kay whether outback women peeled off their clothes to do the housework. She doubted the practice was a common one, and then told me the following, which does illustrate how greatly notions of feminine modesty have altered in the past fifty years or so.

On her verandah early this century Mrs Ronan was entertaining a great friend, Mrs Mac, whom she approved as being 'a very proud and ladylike woman'. Below the verandah railing little Kay Ronan, much too young to be allowed to hear women's confidential talk, hid among the plants to eavesdrop.

They were complaining about the dreadful summer heat. Mrs Mac said 'Mind you I do get a bit of relief for myself at night, though.' 'Oh how?' mum asked eagerly. 'Well,' Mrs Mac bent closer and dropped her voice so it was hard for me, below in the greenery off the verandah, to hear. 'What I do Mrs Ronan, I tell you frankly, is I wring out my thinnest cambric nightie in cold water and slip into that.' Mum made some sort of surprised and shocked noise, but I do know that afterwards *she* tried it, too. I heard her one hot night and lay there trying to imagine how it felt. I know that more women than Mrs Mac and mum tried that trick on hot nights because later on, during a Darwin visit, when I was about seventeen, and so of age to be allowed to listen-in to women's confidences, I heard it quoted as a (*very* private of course) 'wrinkle', passed one to another by *very* reserved ladies indeed. I even heard that Mrs Aeneas Gunn used it for ease, though in her time one would never have indited that fact.

If slang once existed for shocking feminine mysteries of so essentially innocent an order, it has gone far out of date and probably vanished. Or perhaps the slang persists but its original meaning is no longer understood. 'As funny as the bird on Nellie's hat' is quite widespread in current usage, but no one seems to know who Nellie was or why the bird on her hat was any funnier than the once fashionable stuffed (or imitation) birds that perched on many an Edwardian chapeau. Perhaps hat and bird were worn by Nellie Stewart, the stage darling of that era. But the cushion-like piles of hair that supported that extraordinary millinery, and to which it was skewered by hat pins inches long, were combed over a kind of felt base called a 'rat' which I find equally funny.

Some slang usages persist because they are adaptable to altering ways and styles of life. Not only in the outback, but often in cities countless Australian households were chronically short of water. Many places that are closely settled suburbs nowadays did not acquire a mains supply until mid century. Rainwater tanks on stout wooden stands supplied domestic water, and in dry times it was precious. Tank water for washing and baths had to be bucketed into a boiler on the stove or the copper. Affluent households had a tank on the roof to which rainwater could be pumped, and this gave enough pressure for proper baths. Even after coal gas was common in suburbia many households preferred their reliable 'chip heater', clamped to the bath, to a 'gas geyser' which was a temperamental appliance, difficult to light safely and prone to 'blowing out', and also to dribbling verdigris down the plug end of the tub. Whatever the system used, baths were slow to heat and fill, and many families could not afford enough water for a complete bath every day. 'Splitting chips', often from the slats of fruit boxes, was one of the domestic tasks that husbands hated, small boys loathed and avoided if they could, and many a woman performed with weary exasperation. Those of us who 'spit chips' when we are furious perhaps commemorate old annoyance with a small alteration.

On non-bath days people used a tin dish of hot water for ablutions, and kids were instructed to 'wash up as far as possible, down as far as possible, and leave possible till later'. In other words it was sensible hygiene to use the cleanest water for one's face, arms and shoulders, then wash the genital area; it was understood that feet came last. This phrase persists in the slang of some nurses as an answer to a patient who protests the impossibility of achieving comfortable cleanliness from a basin atop a bed-table.

As to a proper bath, children were expected to share the precious hot water, usually in descending order of age. 'Bath order' in many families was as important, and as much a source of contention, as the pecking order among hens.

Women seem to have invented, and been the exclusive users of, several terms for a quick or 'important' wash, whether to conserve water or time. 'A Mary Pickford in three acts' (face/neck, privates, feet) was one of these; a 'whore's bath' and 'to take an APC' (armpits and crotch) were others.

The daughters and granddaughters of those women who went to work in factories, shops and offices found 'to take an APC' a useful equivocal phrase. If you dashed out to the washroom for an APC half an hour before 'knocking-off time' your boss might sympathise with your headache, as he supposed, rather than realise that you were 'beating the gun' to get away quickly from work and meet your boyfriend.

The APC also belongs to an order of Sheilaspeak that allows members of a group who understand it to convey information to each other while excluding men, children or other outsiders. Mary meets Wayne for the first time and 'likes the looks of him' but her friend Kathy, who went to school with Wayne hisses 'WHS!'. It is up to Mary to decide whether she wants to go out with a member of the 'Wandering Hands Society'. Mary, Kathy, Bill and Ron leave work together to walk to the bus stop. Kathy says to Mary 'You lot go on. Don't miss the bus, but I've just remembered I'm out of white bread, and George is calling tonight.' Mary understands that Kathy wants to dash into a chemist shop to buy sanitary napkins. She may choose 'sliced sandwich' (thin size) or 'sliced toast' (thick), or maybe she uses 'fruit cocktails' (tampons) — a cylindrical toffee wrapped in white paper looks very similar.

There are probably as many slang synonyms for menstruation and its appurtenances as there are offices and factories and girls' schools in Australia. 'I'm on me rags' (or 'red rags') is prevalent at the moment, curiously reverting to a time before sanitary napkins were widely available and when strips of towelling and sheets were worn during menstruation. Older generations talk of 'my friend' or 'the curse'.* When Kay Brown was a young bride in Mount Isa she had a rough, tough raucous neighbour called Gloria whom Kay, child of a modest upbringing and trained to regard upper-crust Melbourne usage circa 1900 as the acme of propriety, often could not understand. One elderly man tried to advise her:

'Don't go being all Melbourne snob with old Gloria ... she's rough as bags but sharp, too, and don't you forget her heart's good.'

One morning a passer by, a slap happy what d' y' care sort, called over my front vegie garden, 'Cripes, don't go near her over th' road t'day, she's whipping the cat all over the place!' I mistranslated this as meaning that Gloria was unwell, perhaps with a bad headache and decided to offer help. Over the road I went and asked, 'Aren't you well? A headache?' Gloria, 'a tall Norman Linday-vital shape', glared at me a second and then roared, 'Headache! I'll say I bloody have. Well? No *well* about me. Me bloody visitors 're late!' Off she went, and I returned home, puzzled, but still feeling sorry for the dreaded Gloria, and baked a cake, iced it prettily and took it across the road for a peace offering. 'What's that for?' growled Gloria. 'Well, I thought it might help you. You know, for when your visitors get here.'

You never heard such *yells*! She simply rocked and rolled about yelling with laughter. I stood, rather offended but not sure I understood. Then she wiped her eyes and told me, 'You know what love? None of us 's ever seen what Big Charlie [Kay's husband] ever saw in you. Now I know. You're a bloody laugh a minute, that's what!'

I retired, 'very Melbourne huffily' but that evening Big Charlie explained all. There was a happy ending that made big Glo' a staunch friend of mine. Her tardy 'callers' arrived and she always credited 'that good laugh you give me, love' as 'having done the trick'.

---

*Possibly deriving from Tennyson: 'The curse is come upon me, cried the Lady of Shallot'.

Ladies only

(Ladies Only)

SPACKLE-FILLER, LIPPIE AND A FLAPJACK

Eyes like two holes burned in a blanket
and mouths like the bottom of a bird cage

She dropped a few pegs, had a
re-bore and needed some treatment
in the pipes

A five-finger discount (shoplifting)

'ME DUCHESS IS LOSING HER DRAWERS'

An inter-course cigarette

A CHARITY MOLL OR EA (ENTHUSIASTIC AMATEUR)

'Flapjack'

Only a woman rushes off 'to put on my face' before going out, though some feminine usages and colloquialisms are used by male transvestites who borrow them along with women's clothes, accessories and make-up. First she may apply 'spackle-filler' (foundation make-up), then 'lippie' and powder from her 'flapjack' (powder compact).* She 'runs a comb' through her 'hairdo' and reflects that it's about time she had a fresh 'perm' as she frantically looks for a 'grip' or 'bobbie pin' to restrain a cowlick. If she's the enviable kind of woman whose hair 'behaves itself', rather than the more usual female 'who can't do a thing with it', she may, these days, own a blow-drier and give herself a 'blow-wave' each morning; this invention has superseded the rollers and 'butterfly' grips (metal hair-wavers) which used to sprout from suburban heads and look like surrealist sculpture albeit they were often partly hidden under a scarf.

---

*Dr Margaret Diesendorf, who was born and educated in Austria, says that in 1928-30 Viennese teenage girls used the word 'flapjack' for *Puderdose* (powder box). She adds that 'interestingly *Flappe* is a wry face referring mainly to the shape of the mouth'.

Only women enter the 'Ladies' or 'Powder Room' to 'spend a penny' (urinals for men are free) or to 'wash my hands' or 'powder my nose'.

Both sexes may endure that mysterious affliction known to Australians as 'nerves of the stomach' and, after a heavy night at pub or club, men and women equally might feel as if their eyes were 'like two holes burned in a blanket' or their mouths like 'the bottom of a bird cage'. But women only 'get caught', are 'let down' or 'fall', and endure 'tube trouble' or 'womb collapse'.

Among 'the girls' (girls being women friends of any age up to senility) gynaecological and surgical gossip remains popular. Often meanings are conveyed as much by facial expression or nuances of speech as by words. One woman mentioned in a letter that during her childhood the overheard phrase 'She's had her tonsils out' invariably referred to any major operation. A woman might have 'dropped a few pegs', 'had a re-bore' or need treatment 'in the pipes'. 'Mummy's going in [to hospital] for a little op', might indicate a simple curettage or be a euphemism for abortion; men more often spoke of women 'having the boilers scraped down'. Other synonyms include 'slip a joey', 'crack an egg', 'need a scrape' (which can be a curette recommended for other reasons), or 'have appendicitis'. This last example is equivocal Sheilaspeak; with the co-operation of a sympathetic 'medico' it can be used to excuse absence from work or unaccountable illness.

Lactating mothers can make the unique choice to keep the baby's feed 'where the cat can't get at it'. It is only women (and those, perhaps, of Cornish descent, for they are invariably miners' wives) who describe a baby that is not truly ill, but not thriving, as 'teasy'.

'Boddies' or bodices, 'chimmies', 'pettis', 'slips', 'scanties', 'drawers' and 'pinnies' are worn only by females, though children of both sexes may have 'a pain in the pinny', and both sexes wear 'long Johns,' 'coms' or 'combies' (combinations). 'Leos' (leotards or long tights) are also popular winter wear for women; like 'nylons', whether stockings or panty-hose, they are

36

Cardie

prone to 'snags' that lead to ladders and to 'pilling'. (Pills, which also form on woollen fabrics, are little balls of fibre that form on surfaces, especially after prolonged or careless washing.)

Nothing is cosier on a cold night than a nice knitted or crocheted 'hugmetight' around the shoulders of your 'nightie' though, at a pinch, a 'cardie' will serve. Nowadays panty-hose have largely superseded 'roll-ons' or 'step-ins' (suspender belts), but 'control briefs' are often worn to restrain fleshy bulges, and some panty-hose have 'control tops'. The 'merry widow', a corselet or belt designed to pinch in the waist, came in with Dior's 'new-look' fashions of the 1940s and remained to torture all but the slimmest of girls until the early 1960s.

It is not easy to decide whether certain fashion terms are slang or, rather, descriptive terms for kinds of clothes and decoration that come and go with fashion itself. A peplum is a peplum, a stole a stole, a puffed sleeve a puffed sleeve. But other terms, sometimes deriving from brand names, 'catch on' and are used for garments that could easily be described in another way, or called something different. 'Witches' britches' are a case in point.

'Witches' britches' were winter garments of the mini-skirt era.

Made of brightly coloured warm-knit nylon and trimmed with lace, these tight-fitting pants peeped under short skirts. Bolder spirits had hearts, monograms or other devices, embroidered on one leg of the britches just above the lace. One woman school-teacher of that time intercepted a note that read, 'Let's go to C—'s (a chain store) after school and snitch some witches' britches.' To shoplift is to get 'a five finger discount'.

An outmoded feminine slang word was reported by a New South Wales woman whose grandmother, a strict Methodist lady, died aged ninety-four in the 1920s.

Until she died my grandmother would not wear ordinary 'bloomers' (as they were called by the 1920s) so her daughters still had to make her traditional pants which (vulgarly) were known as 'free traders'. They comprised knee-length calico pants trimmed with lace but, instead of a front and back seam, were open from the front waist to the back waist, and fastened *around* the waist by long tapes. It meant you could use the toilet without pulling your pants down.

The woman who has to stop scrubbing the floor or weeding the garden when unexpected visitors arrive and 'turns around' to 'run up' a batch of scones and 'throw them' in the oven seems to be using exclusively Australian terms. As for talented girls who can 'run up a dress' ...

It is astonishing that the 'duchess' has been overlooked in compilations of Australian slang. If every duchess set that has been embroidered with lazy daisies or crocheted in lacy patterns were laid end to end, the arrangement would cross and re-cross the Nullarbor or, perhaps more appropriately, outline the coast of the Gulf of Carpentaria, for it is chiefly in Queensland that a dressing-table is called a duchess, though nation-wide a runner and two flanking small mats is known as a duchess set. Once, in a Queensland pub with flimsy walls between bedrooms, a mystified southerner heard a loud crash from the adjoining room that was shared by two seasonal workers, followed by some furious swearing and then, 'Wake up and help, Blue. Me duchess is losing her drawers'.*

Arduous Feminine Task No: 35

Running up a dress.

---

*I mentioned the 'duchess' as a peculiarly Queensland usage to a group of Rockhampton girls, one of whom asked, in a very puzzled way, 'Well what else *would* you call it?'

Women have a particular emphasis in their voices when they say, of some man or other who has infuriated them, 'He's thick!' Men who behave insensitively or badly are accused of having their minds only 'on their bellies and what's hanging off them', and of dreary marriages it is said that 'women put up with sex to get marriage and men put up with marriage to get sex'.

A widely used Australian term for the sexual act is 'to have a naughty', but one religious lady, circa 1930s, referred to intercourse as 'a naught'. This irony was probably unintended since she was the contented wife of an affectionate husband. A story is told of one clergyman's wife whose daughter invited a young man home for dinner. The mother wanted to indicate her broad-mindedness to this guest whom she considered rather worldly, and, as she cleared the meat dishes from the table, and substituted pudding plates, she set an ashtray beside his place and invited him to enjoy 'an inter-course cigarette'.

Venereal disease makes no gender distinctions but only women exhibit a symptom known as 'the whites' (which may have non-specific causes). But while pubescent boys welcome the appearance of body hair few girls desire 'a forest' or 'mohair stockings', and will assiduously 'mow the lawn' to control them. Feminine pubic hair is 'a thicket'.

Who but a woman would complain that a man is a 'linen lifter', or is 'trying to pirate me' or 'put on the hard word' or 'get me into the bushes/scrub/mulga'?

One country family spoke of anyone taking a big risk as 'doing what the girl did', it being understood that the girl 'fell in'. In this same family, someone voicing mock displeasure would say, 'Ahrrr, give me my hat and pants!' The phrase derived from a story often told by one of their aunts in warning tones — aunty plainly missed the point of the joke. A girl who was displeased by her boyfriend's importunate behaviour in a park at night exclaimed, 'Give me my hat and pants, I'm going home.'

A similar story from the same period, circa 1940s, concerned a young man who, with the help of his girlfriend, was polishing his car. He needed a soft cloth to complete the job and asked, 'What do you do with your pants when you wear them out?' 'I wear them home if I can find them.'

During World War II Australian girls who wore long, elaborately dressed 'pompadour' hair styles were said by some of their disapproving sisters to be 'dangling Yank bait'.

The slang of prostitutes (prostitution is 'cracking it') alters constantly. But even in such a group, in Australia, a few old English low-life words seem to remain current perpetually although with subtle alterations to definition and emphasis. One example is 'moll'. To some Australians 'moll' has an affectionate connotation very puzzling to non-Australians or to locals who do not understand the conventions of certain unconventional speakers. (This usage is akin to the way Australian males intend words like 'bastard' and 'bugger' to be terms of friendship and acceptance.) At present a 'charity moll' is the equivalent of a World War II 'EA' or 'enthusiastic amateur': a promiscuous woman whose sexual favours are theoretically not available for sale, or not for honest sale for an agreed cash payment. A charity moll barters herself, instead, for presents, dinners, theatre and show tickets. 'Working women' or women 'in the trade' (prostitutes) have a deep scorn for charity molls not so much because they represent a threat to business, but because they delude themselves and are not prepared to admit that they are just as 'bad' as a harlot, or conversely that any harlot is as good as they are. The dividing line is cold cash. Prostitutes, rightly or wrongly, accuse charity molls of being responsible for spreading venereal disease because they *are* amateurs. Interestingly, venereal disease retains its very old generic term, 'the pox'.

Prostitutes, too, have other strong feelings that are mirrored by language. At present to work in a 'massage parlor' is regarded as professional; to work the streets is not. To work in or conduct a parlor carries connotations of professionalism and self respect that the word 'brothel' is denied by the women themselves.

In degree at least, women are distinguished from charity molls if they provide 'an after dinner mint' to men who expect, and ask for, this sweet conclusion to an expensive night out. The implication is that 'minters' are less promiscuous, and more often are 'going steady' with their men.

41

4

Telling it like it isn't

'HE WAS ALL OVER ME LIKE A RASH'

Toffy and tossles

The little girl's room

cunning as a lavvy rat

BND (BLOODY NEAR DEAD, NURSING SLANG)

Youse

A TOUCH OF THE TAR BRUSH

All piddle and wind like the
barber's cat

Bangs like a dunny door in a gale

A young woman publisher from Melbourne went to work in London about ten years ago and was astonished to discover that her new colleagues found her idiomatic language extraordinarily varied and colourful. Soon after her arrival she accepted a dinner invitation from a man she had just met and next morning, with annoyance, reported at the office that he 'was all over me like a rash'. This was greeted with amusement and interest, though it seemed an everyday remark to her and would seem common enough to most Australians. Although this woman had never considered her repertoirc and use of colloquialisms to be extensive she soon found that it was indeed remarkable among her English friends.

Whether or not our slanguage is richer than others in the English-speaking world, or whether we commonly use colloquial speech more often and widely than people in other countries, I have no idea. Certainly, if everyone spoke with absolute correctness and pedantry we might often understand each other better because, undeniably, a good deal of what gives colour to language also makes bricks for the tower of Babel.

Euphemisms and genteelisms, whether slangy or straightforward, add to the confusion. When I was a social worker in a large city hospital a physician who was examining a sick baby was called to the telephone. While he was absent the baby's mother 'took a peep' at the card he was filling in and nearly 'blew her top'. Surely, she yelled for all to hear, a doctor of all people ought to understand that any baby might have a 'cackie nappy'. There was no need for him to be downright rude about it. What the doctor had scribbled, was not 'Pooh' as the woman wrongly thought, but a common abbreviation: PUO (Pyrexia [fever] of Unknown Origin).

James Meagher, an Irish-born solicitor who practised law in Sydney reported the following confused exchange which he heard at the Police Court in Liverpool Street, Sydney in 1948, offered as extenuating evidence by Mrs Jones who was charged with assaulting Mrs Smith and giving her a black eye and bruised jaw. A street in Darlinghurst's red light area had for a long while resounded to the disputes of these two antagonists, and a policeman who knew them well told the court that Mrs Jones was frequently irritated by Mrs Smith's allegedly 'stuck up' and 'toffy' way of speaking. Mrs Jones was then called to the witness box:

So there she [Mrs Smith] comes walking along the footpath and when she seen me she tried to hide what she was carrying but blind Freddie could tell it was a bottle pushed down into her shopping bag. 'And where are you off to at this time of morning?' I ask nicely.

'Down to the surgery to see the Doc,' she says; cagey but.

'Oh really! With a bottle!!??'

'Yes,' says she, 'it's you-rine' says she.

'Y' *what?*' says I.

'You-rine' says she.

'*My what?*??' says I.

'Oh ... piss,' says she.

'Shit!!' says I, and that's how the stoush started.

Toff

Euphemisms and genteelisms are nowhere more rampant than in the nursery. With the best will in the world even the most enlightened of parents find it nearly impossible to avoid using them. Those of the Dr Spock generation consciously scorned old-fashioned usages like 'num nums' for breasts, and when pregnant did not speak of being 'happy eventing' or 'infanticipating'. A penis was called a penis and not a 'tossle' or a 'doodle'. Babies were babies, not 'bubbas'.

This was all very well, but from the moment these infants stumbled their first few steps distant from their parents' sole care they were forced to learn many of the words and phrases so well-meaningly eschewed — otherwise they couldn't communicate either with older people or with their own contemporaries from less 'advanced' families. I shall never forget the lack of comprehension on the face of a squirming child when

Num — Nums

a kindly elderly neighbour enquired, 'Do you want to do wee wee?' The child wriggled in misery. 'Do you want to go to toilie?' The child stood in a puddle.

The language of bodily functions must be learned at several levels and re-learned several times in an ordinary life span. A 'kiddilywinks' or 'pipsqueak' must acquire the vocabularies of mum, dad and siblings, two pairs of grandparents, assorted uncles, aunts and cousins, baby-sitters, neighbours and above all of other children. A two-year-old who sits its 'bottie' on its 'pottie' to 'do pee pee' meets another who 'goes to the toilet' to 'wee wee'. If they are boys one may call his penis a 'tossle' and the other a 'doodle' or 'willie'. A girl's genitals and urinary area is her 'front tottie', her anus is the 'back tottie', and this term may also apply to a boy's anus. One child 'does its business', talks of 'binnie one' or 'binnie two' or 'number one' and 'number two', and another 'makes cackie', or 'poop'.

For some inexplicable reason 'snot' for nasal mucus is not considered particularly vulgar in Australia though 'a booboo' or 'a booby' is preferred in the nursery.

The word 'toilet' used to be considered a dreadful genteelism by Australians with pretensions to plain usage, they preferred lavatory, which is itself a euphemism. 'Toilet' won and became universal, though it is considered very 'in' in some circles to revert to words like 'dunny' and 'sh'ouse' (from 'shit-house'), or to adopt overseas terms such as 'loo' or 'john'.* 'Going to Mary's room' or 'going to visit Mary' or 'aunty' are examples of a range of euphemisms used by some women — the proper names vary widely. 'The little girls' room' is still heard of. 'To have a leak' or 'to make water' seem to be exclusively male usages.

Now 'toilet' is generally adopted secondary euphemisms have followed. People who might once have complained about dogs fouling footpaths talk about 'dogs using the footpath as a toilet' or 'going to the toilet on the footpath'. This range of euphemism reached a nadir of absurdity when in April 1981 an ABC radio news item mentioned a group of children from an outer sub-urban school who wrote personal letters to the Premier of New South Wales complaining about sub-standard buildings and facilities. One child explained that 'someone missed out on her lunch because a possum went to the toilet on it'.

Yet if euphemisms and genteelisms were abandoned entirely a range of humour that depends on *double entendre* and varying levels of apprehension would vanish. As most Australians know the enduring popularity of the dog on the tucker box at Gunda-gai, a famous sculpture notwithstanding, is not because the dog faithfully sat guarding the tucker box, but because it shat on its master's 'crib'.

Some euphemisms have wit in their own right. An old Sydney term for breaking wind was 'a one o'clock', deriving from the cannon that used to be fired from Fort Denison, a harbour island whose original and still popular name was 'Pinchgut'. A woman who grew up in Tasmania during the 1920s recalls her father's term for a corpse; a 'wombat', which is rhyming slang for *hors de combat*.

Other euphemisms approach trade or professional jargon. American medical slang has several terms intended, at least to some extent, to spare relatives of patients concern or grief —

*On a radio phone-in session after I asked for slang examples a young woman said 'cunning as a toilet rat' was a phrase her family used when she was a small child. The compere said 'Really', and she laughed, 'Well actually we used to say "cunning as a lavvy rat".'

MFC on a chart, for instance, means to the initiated 'measure for coffin'. An Australian nursing term, BND, which stands for 'bloody near dead', may have similar connotations, but many terms used by Australian nurses are probably closer to a shared group language. One nurse who wrote said that BND and similar terms are not used with intentional disrespect but rather to bring 'a sense of humour into a situation that can be emotionally traumatic for the staff if allowed to be too involved'.

Among these colloquialisms are 'aggro', an aggressive patient; 'dunny', a confused, disorientated and (usually) senile patient; a 'stiff dunny' is dead or, in other words 'has carked it', and a patient who has 'sloughed off' has disappeared. A confused patient may also be 'away with the fairies', 'ga-ga', 'doe-doe', 'dumbo', 'dubbo' or have 'lost 'is marbles'. 'Geris' are geriatric patients but *also* may be rigid and unpopular senior nurses. Some symptoms are 'supratentorial' — all in the mind. Patients *en masse* are 'the happy family'. A 'Super D' is a derelict or alcoholic; a hopeless person has 'packed up'. A nurse assigned to give an enema or suppository is a 'goldfinger'; a person trained to take blood samples is a 'vampire' or 'blood sucker'. 'Dicky ticker' is a bad heart *or* a person with heart disease; the 'Big C' or 'CA' is cancer; 'the land of the one-sided people' is

Away with the fairies . . .

a rehabilitation ward for stroke patients; 'Ward 13' is the morgue. A psychiatric hospital is a 'shrink klink', 'giggle bin', 'nut factory' or 'peanut factory'. There are racist overtones to the 'Mediterranean syndrome', an over-emotional patient or performance; the 'Mediterranean back', which denotes derisive suspicion about a back-ache and 'Mediterranean gut-ache', usually shortened to 'MGA' which is just as suspect as the back-ache.

Mispronunciations, grammatical errors and mistaken use of words occasionally win a true place in colloquial speech. This place has to be distinguished from words whose mis-usage becomes so widely accepted that their new meaning enters acceptable educated language. Examples of the latter might be 'democratic', which was a pejorative term in mid-nineteenth century Australia; 'prestigious', which is now generally accepted as meaning having prestige, and 'enormity' which is increasingly used as a synonym for vastness and not as denoting an outrage. The sort of misuses I have in mind, however, are never likely to enter official language though many people suppose them to be correct. Examples would be 'bronical', a common mispronunciation of bronchial, with its peculiar cousin, 'bronical ectasies' for that least ecstatic of diseases, Bronchiectasis. 'Youse' is another instance.

An Australian writer who is justly successful and respected had very little schooling. In his late teens, aware that his pronunciation and reading were defective, he joined an amateur theatre group whose members recognised his qualities and creative talent and helped him in many ways. After a script meeting one woman quietly drew him aside and said, 'Phil (as I shall call him) you really must stop addressing the group as *youse*. It's quite wrong.' 'Oh no,' Phil said, 'if I speak to you, you're you. If I speak to several people, they're "youse".'

Australian women, more often than men, perhaps, have a penchant for ending statements with 'but'. 'I had a dreadful session with the dentist this morning, it's been a nice day, but.' 'Only snags for tea and a nice half caulie, but.' In central Queensland 'eh' or 'ay' is substituted for 'but', and on a rising inflection. 'Blah, blah, blah' is often used, again I think, particularly by women, as a substitute for etcetera, etcetera. Usually, it is a short-cut in reporting an event or conversation, but it also covers for some dialogue or sequence of happenings that the speaker cannot precisely remember. Either, 'He said he'd do it, but he never did, not the whole weekend, and his excuses! You know, "blah, blah, blah" till I could've screamed, but'; or 'So she told me the whole thing, how she got on the train, and found she'd lost her purse, and tried to explain to the "clippie" (ticket examiner) who wouldn't take her word for it, and blah blah blah till finally she insisted on seeing the station-master.'

In some contexts certain words and phrases describing drunkenness, stupidity, eccentricity, actual insanity and other 'unfortunate' states approach euphemism and genteelism. A woman who would never allege directly that members of certain Australian and New Zealand families had co-habited with Aborigines and Maoris, used to whisper conspiratorially 'of course there's a touch of the tar brush in her/their background'. When I worked in an inner-city public hospital I gained tremendous respect for the conversational stratagems which women adopted to protect their own pride, and to hinder outsiders from guessing the domestic or marital violence they suffered. Prostitutes would aver that a black eye and bruised body were caused by their collision with a door or piece of furniture, or a fall downstairs; wives covered up for drunken husbands and sons. The Casualty Department expected a regular post-weekend tally of 'Monday morning shiners'. Those were brave women, who 'wouldn't say die till a dead horse kicked them', even when they felt like 'six pennyworth of God Help You' or 'last week's Irish stew'. In extenuation of ill treatment they would explain that 'he' was 'full as a tick (or boot)' or came home 'all piddle and wind like the barber's cat' and in the sort of mood that 'I'd get the blame if the cat had kittens'.

The gallantry underlying some feminine and domestic colloquial speech merits both tribute and sympathetic understanding, but this is not the place to discuss the incidence of domestic abuse, assault, cruelty and exploitation as these affect women. The emphasis in several collections of our slang makes it unequivocally plain that Australians find endless humour in coarse ocker expressions, but the other side of coinages like 'sink the sausage' and 'bangs like a dunny door in a gale' is spurious and pays out despair and disaster to many women and children.

5

Fun and games

A BIT OF A HIT AND GIGGLE

Runs like a hairy goat

White Leghorn Day (Ladies' day at bowls)

The Trifecta

THE WANDERING HANDS SOCIETY

One-armed bandits

My father and Judge S— of the New South Wales
Supreme Court, shared the judging of our school
swimming sports relying entirely on their eyesight.
I do not recall any dissent from their decisions; the only rules
were that competitors must swim in a straight line and use the
appropriate stroke for the race. When either judge, or both of
them, had a daughter competing the sports-mistress took over
and Judge S— fired her starting pistol; dad swore off firearms
on 11 November 1918.

How different by the 1960s when my children attended primary school. Annual swimming sports were held in an olympic
pool and supervised by a mother who had been an olympic
swimmer. Many of the children were driven daily to this pool
to train between 5 and 7 a.m. and competed regularly in club
competitions. A judge, with stopwatch, was assigned to each
lane. A child who incorrectly turned, or violated any other of
the numerous rules, was disqualified instantly. Winners of heats
only qualified for the finals if they attained a minimum time.
Passionate parents barracked furiously and frequently disputed
decisions.

These occasions were over-competitive, distasteful, light on sportsmanship and only slightly more acceptable than junior rugby games when mums of seven-year-olds raced up and down the sidelines yelling, 'Get in there Barry, and murder 'im!' or 'Oh-me-gawd, wouldn't that rip the saddle out of y' nightie!'; an exclamation that mystified me until 'that'd rip the saddle off your nightmare' was contributed as an example of Familyspeak.

Several women sent me examples of sporting terms that nostalgically recall vanished eras when amateurs played games just for fun. Escalating land values and proliferating swimming pools have put an end to most private tennis courts. The standard of domestic tennis used to vary greatly. Keen players who played competition tennis at weekends appreciated the opportunity for 'a bit of a hit' or 'knock' to keep in practice before or after work on week-days. If no better partner were available one of the kids lobbed ball after ball to the practiser. Groups of women friends who met regularly and played well on a court

GET IN THERE BARRY, MURDER 'EM! YOU CAN DO IT!

Lollipop tennis

in someone's garden might jokingly refer to these non-tournament games as a 'hit and giggle', a term that in the 1940s supplanted the earlier 'lollipop tennis'. Both these terms applied to unserious and often inept 'backyard tennis' players. Pipsqueaks too young for 'kinder' accompanied their mothers and could be useful chasers of balls that vanished into shrubbery. Players used wooden racquets strung with gut and known as 'bats' with which they 'popped the ball' (a lob) and aced the opposition with any shot they couldn't return. In those lost times golf clubs were called 'sticks' and the adventurous few who visited the snowfields pronounced skis and skiing as 'shees and sheeing'.

Women who might once have enjoyed backyard tennis now play lawn bowls in all-white uniforms and, since bowling clubs, and some golf clubs, segregate the sexes, Ladies' Day at the bowling club is 'White Leghorn Day'.

One correspondent supplied a list of terms used in family cricket games. Some of these terms are used in professional cricketing circles also:

Blob	no runs
Golden blob	out to first ball bowled to batswoman

59

Pair of specs	no runs in both innings
Dorothy Dix	a six
Cheesy kisses	a missed catch

This list of golfing colloquialisms is from Western Australia:

Golf club	bat, waddy
Flagstick	pin, needle
Divot (large)	kipper
Sand bunker	pot, trap, beach

Bad shots

Very high shot		angel bruiser
Very low shot		worm raper, daisy cutter
Hitting the ground first		fat
Hitting the ground with the lower edge of the club, giving a low, scudding shot		thin

Good shots

Long shot	boomer
Long hitter	gorilla
Easy course	diddy bum course

Before TV, scrabble and electronic games, families played card games together. According to the woman who shared her card-playing Familyspeak, these terms date from the 1930s:

Poker terms included Three Tens declared as 'Thirty days' or 'Judge Curlewis',* three Queens declared as 'Three bank clerks'; a pair of threes and a pair of twos were 'Lousies and scabbies' or 'Rats and mice'; and Aces were 'Bullets'.

---

*Judge Herbert Raine Curlewis, 1869-1942. When he retired from the District Court bench in 1939 he was described as 'the greatest judge who ever sat in that jurisdiction'. His son, Adrian, was also a judge of the District Court. H. C. Curlewis's wife was Ethel Turner, author of *Seven Little Australians*.

WORM RAPER!

When my father played crib [cribbage] and his score was two pairs he always called them 'Morgan's Orchard'. I didn't know who Morgan was.

Betting on sport and especially on the 'gee gees' has long been a popular Australian way of separating a fool from his or her money. Both sexes bet, but only women, I think, have a 'flutter'. Both patronise the TAB (Totalizator Agency Board) often known as 'th' tab'. When a chosen horse 'runs like a hairy goat'

61

both sexes 'do their dough' or, as a Queensland cattleman's wife often had cause to exclaim, 'I've done me arse' (she pronounced it *arz*). A frequently disappointed uncle is remembered for his dejected explanation for failure to back a winner: 'I could've, should've, would've but just didn't.'

A Sydney woman said of a friend's daughter that she had won the daily double but missed out on the trifecta: the young woman in question was having her wedding at the fashionable St Marks, Darling Point, the reception at the Royal Sydney Yacht Squadron, but had missed out on the honeymoon in Fiji.

In the 1950s and 60s the Albert Palais at Leichhardt, a Sydney suburb, lent its name to a dance called the 'Albert Crawl'; the correspondent who told me this said the Palais was frequented by members of the Wandering Hands Society, as many dance-halls were. Most of them have disappeared together with the famed Sydney 'Troc' (the Trocadero) which was an immense city ballroom where countless Sydney debs curtseyed to countless Lady Mayoresses and wives of State Governors. Regular public dances were held there, also. Altered liquor-licensing laws were one of the factors that led to the demise of the dance-hall where regular Friday and Saturday night 'hops' were held. Tavern licences permit evening drinking and entertainment in hotels and pubs and bistro-style venues. In New South Wales, proliferating licensed clubs, largely financed by 'the pokies' or 'one-armed bandits' offer galaxies of attractions, including dance nights.

Numerous citizens feared that relaxed licensing laws would lead to general drunkenness, but many people, young and old, are now happy to order soft drinks and fruit juices on licensed premises and, among younger age groups and family parties, the traditional compulsion to 'shout' rounds of drinks seems to be disappearing. Barmaids fail to 'bat an eyelid' when customers who would once have thought it impossibly juvenile or 'poofterish' to order anything lighter than beer, ask for a small white wine in a long glass to be filled with soda, or orange drink, or soda and bitters, or a Coke. Also of the past are notices like the one I saw in 1946 in a country pub: 'No kids, dogs or women in this bar'.

6

A goose's bridle: Amulets against the world

TAKE YOUR FEET OFF YOUR BODY

London Fog, the bludger that
never lifts

A hand like a foot and a foot like
a hand and a face like a
howey—doodle

Dandy grey russet — the colour of a
field mouse's tit

THINGIMMYBOB HANDICAP

Private jokes and family sayings are an extension of domestic privacy. They are among those substances that lead to blood being thicker than water; they give permanence and stability to the family group. My family mystifies a visitor with an expression that, to show friendship, is then explained. Years ago my husband helped an elderly Mr Malaprop to paint his flat on a very hot day. Mr M. made a large jug of cold lemonade and then called, 'Come down off that ladder and take your feet off your body!' In our family parlance 'take your feet off your body' substitutes for 'take your weight off your feet', to the understandable puzzlement of outsiders.

One factor that contributes to the popularity of many a family-saga novel or film is the reiterated private phrase. 'Nobody tells me anything' grumbles Galsworthy's Uncle James Forsyte, in *The Forsyte Saga*, and we more readily identify with that clan as we recognise one of our own tedious but well-loved kinsfolk. Enduring friendships between people of all ages, as well as love affairs and good marriages, partly depend upon this kind of group give and take, and a family is a group.

Some Australian nicknames are widespread, but others seem to be confined to families. Generations of one Sydney family have dubbed successive local gossips 'Cold Meat Maggie': she stays out too late to prepare a decent meal for her family and is a close relative of 'London Fog', the bludger who never lifts.

Mythical personalities or nonsense phrases for people and things whose names are forgotten or elusive are very common: 'Whose-me-whatsit', 'thingmegig', 'oojar-capivio' or 'whatcha-macallit' (which can also refer to an object — 'she uses a clever little thingmegig or whatchamacallit for unpicking stitches'), 'whoflickie', 'whasmigig', '(Mrs) Fizzgig', (Mr) Marsoolacoopa', and the mother of them all, which is attributed to a Sydney mother-in-law, 'Sarah-Jane-Myra-Ranonawich'. One woman reported that her family's reply to a question to which there is no answer is 'Whosimijar and obamatitty'.

A cartoon by Low, purchased by my father, is one of the earliest pictures I remember. I do not know in which journal it originally appeared — the *Bulletin* perhaps. The picture is of two rather dopey looking punters dressed foppishly; the race-course fashions worn by a woman in the background suggest a date circa 1919. One fop says to his friend, 'Awful ass that fellow Whats-his-name. Told him specially to put something on What-dyer-call-it for the Thingimmybob Handicap and dashed if he

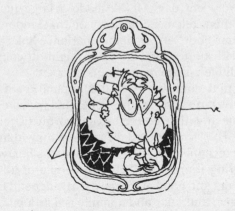

Sara-Jane-Myra-Ranonawich

66

didn't forget all about it.' The title of the cartoon, appropriately, is 'Some silly asses are so forgetful'.

The origin of some phrases common in Familyspeak has been forgotten. Many Australians on a warm day in late winter, and especially if the first 'blowie' of the season buzzes around the kitchen, remark that 'Spring is sprung'. One Sydney family knows the whole verse and recites it antiphonally using an exaggerated Yankee accent that presumably indicates its origin:

> Spring is sprung! The grass is riz!
> I wonder where the boydies is?
> The little boyds is on the wing.
> Why! How absoyd!
> *(All together)* We always hoyd the little wings
> Was on the boyd!

Another family, since at least the 1890s, has perpetuated this curious phrase to describe someone who looks odd or peculiar: 'A hand like a foot and a foot like a hand and a face like a howey-doodle'. The woman who wrote this out for me said, 'Whatever a howey-doodle may be, or how one should spell it we never learned, but it was always pronounced with an imitation brogue so perhaps it had an Irish origin.'

A family of Cornish and Scottish descent who came to Australia from New Zealand has used several strange phrases for generations. A nondescript colour, impossible to describe, is 'dandy grey russet — the colour of a field mouse's tit'. A term of approval meaning 'very good indeed' in response to the question, 'What do you think of ...?' is 'Damn the better since Leather Arse died.'

A Sydney woman of sixty, a younger member of a large family, her eldest brother being eighty, wrote, 'One strange, silly quoted saying, which I've never heard outside our family, but which I'm assured was not invented by any of us ... it had to be repeated as rapidly as possible, while enunciating clearly and using as

67

much dramatic expression as one could muster: A man said "You're mad." I said, "Mad?" He said, "Yes." I said, "Who?" He said, "You!" I said, "Me?" He said, "Yes." I said, "No!"'

While I was working on this book 'a wigwam for a goose's bridle', even more than the 'lily on the dustbin', became a talisman: a phrase that both exemplifies and symbolises the atavistic depths and currents of the folk mind. It fascinated me because of its mystery, apparent antiquity, and the strangeness of its Australian popularity. Although it is one of the most used and widespread of all snubs and put-downs to children in Australia, and although it almost certainly originated in Britain or Ireland, perhaps in the sixteenth or seventeenth century, it does not seem to have survived in its country of origin to anything like the extent it remains in colloquial speech in Australia.

Its meaning is a puzzle, and so are its variant forms. Is it a 'wigwam', 'wing wong', or 'whim wham'? Is it a 'bridle' or 'bridal'? Was the goose, which firmly remains the constant noun about which variants revolve, a respectable nursery goose or a prostitute? 'Goose' was an Elizabethan cant phrase for a whore, and 'Winchestergoose' was a venereal disease.* By association, how respectable were Old Mother Goose and Goosey Goosey Gander? Quicksands may underlie many a wholesome crust of nursery lore.

Fairly early in my collecting 'a wigwam for a goose's bridle' appeared in letters, usually from New South Wales. This was the form spoken in my husband's Brisbane childhood, and in mine in Sydney; in those words we replied when our own children pestered us to know 'What are you knitting? Sewing? Cutting out on the work-bench?' or asked about the contents of some mysterious package. This is how most people remember the phrase being used. A few early correspondents gave the variant 'wing wong' instead of 'wigwam'; for a time I did not

---

*A 'goose' is also a tailor's smoothing iron, the handle of which resembles a goose's neck. Shakespeare made a pun on the word in *Macbeth*, Act II, scene 3: 'Come in tailor, here you may roast your goose.'

realise the importance of that variant. One mother who grew up in Moonta, South Australia, in the 1870s or 1880s, answered the question 'What is it?' or 'What are you making?' with 'a wing wong handle for the mustard pot'.

Then a woman wrote that, in her family, 'a wigwam for a goose's bridle' was sometimes, but not always, followed by 'to chase the sun up and down', and a man reported 'a whim wong for a goose's bridle for winding up the sun'. These additions appealed to my imagination and set me off on, well, a wild goose chase. The pictures they formed in my mind's eye were of a Daedalus-like hero who harnesses a goose to chase the sun and between its wings erects a shelter, a tent, a wigwam, to shield himself from the sun's fierce heat. The trouble with this theory was twofold; none of the experts in children's literature whom I consulted knew of any such myth or fairytale, and, also, 'wing wong' began to appear so often in reports of the phrase that its claims could be disregarded no longer.

At this point, on Mike Carlton's 2GB Sydney radio show, I referred to the mysterious 'wigwam' and, rather wistfully, observed that although most Australians know it, none seem to have any idea of its meaning. Mike Carlton subsequently mentioned the puzzle in his column in the *Sun Herald*. Then feathers really began to fly as people wrote to me, and to Carlton, pressing the claims of 'wing wong' against 'wigwam' and 'whim wham' (or 'wim wam') against both.

A man of seventy-three who is descended from two arrivals by the First Fleet in January 1788, wrote that his father used 'wigwam' about seventy years ago. Another writer, whose mother used 'wigwam' seventy-odd years ago, was surprised when he saw the phrase in print with the usage 'whim wham'. He wrote, 'I have the impression the expression is a quotation, but I can't say where it's lifted from.' He had taken the trouble, however, to look up *Roget's Thesaurus* where 'I find whim wham listed with toy, geegaw, bauble, trinket, bagatelle, kicksaw, knickknack, trifle, "trifle's light as air"'.

The *Shorter Oxford Dictionary* shows that 'whim wham' was reported first in 1529 and frequently referred to a trifle of dress.

It does not list 'wing wong'. The English language has used 'wig-wam', an American-Indian tent-like shelter, since the seventeenth century, but I suspect the word was only widely current after Longfellow's poem 'Hiawatha' became popular. 'Hiawatha' was published first in 1855. I would guess that towards the end of the nineteenth century 'wigwam' took over from 'wing wong' and 'whim wham' in some Australian families.

One of the people who responded to Mike Carlton's publicity was Neville Evans, a passionate crusader for 'wing wong' and also an energetic protagonist, even at this late date, for justice for Ben Hall, a bushranger who was shot by police in 1865. Mr Evans's first letter — quoted here with his permission — was unequivocally anti-wigwam.

Either I have some good or bad news for Nancy Keesing in regards to the old saying 'a wig-wam for a goose's bridle'. That supposed saying, was *never* a wig-wam, but A WING WONG FOR A GOOSE'S BRIDLE! This expression was handed down from my grandfather, grandmother, and then from my mother to myself.

They first heard the expression in approx. 1877 when 'Bold Ben Hall' held up my grandparents' hotel in TARAGO, not far from Goulburn. Ben Hall and three of his bushrangers entered the hotel and Ben placed his pistol on the bar counter and demanded a flask of rum and food. My grandmother was nursing my mother in the bar at that time and she tried to excuse herself from cooking a meal as she was nursing her child. Ben told her to give the baby to him and cook the gang some ham and eggs. My grandmother complied and Ben gave the baby back to my grandmother when she returned with the food. He gave my mother back and at the same time looking at the food and then the baby, said — 'Fair exchange, a wing wong for a goose's bridle!'

They finished their meal and big Ben ordered another flask of rum and put two gold sovereigns on the counter and they took off. Neither (*sic*) my grandparents [ever] forgot that expression and it was written in my grandfather's diary and then passed on to my mother.

I was born in Goulburn 17th April, 1917, and [when] I turned twelve years of age, I had the chance of reading that diary and I will never forget those very words, as my Mother used that expression fairly often during her lifetime.

Perceptive readers will by now have noticed that, since Ben Hall died in 1865, the date given for this incident cannot be correct. I will return to this point shortly, but first I want to quote another interesting part of this letter which discusses the phrase against a background of the old Bourke Street (Sydney) Public School where Neville Evans was a student:

The expression a 'wing wong for a goose's bridle' was used quite often by my elder brothers and sisters and I have never forgotten it, and even my Headmaster, Mr Patrick (Pat) Wigg ... used the expression himself. It was never Wigwam as he would have cut my bloody throat if he heard me use an expression implying his name — Wigg. I studied Hiawatha at that age of 14, and I would have punned on the expression Wigg *wham*! He used to love me and broke his favourite cane over my shoulder and my brother Ken came down to school and flattened him. So where do we go from here?

Mr Evans further emphasised his point by saying that he kept pigeons as pets and called his favourite pigeon 'Bronze wing wong'. In subsequent correspondence with Mr Evans he apologised for the confusion with dates and said his mother was born *late* in 1863 at Tarago near Goulburn. His grandfather's name was ('Honest') John Horton and his grandmother's first name was Margaret. Honest John, as well as keeping a hotel at Tarago, drove a Cobb and Co. coach. He tells, too, how he was 'ragged' at school about his mother's infant meeting with the bushranger, 'but I didn't give one damn in hell'.

Several other people wrote suggesting that the mystery phrase may have been Irish in origin, usually on the basis that they heard it used by people of Irish descent, but I think that is coincidental; it was certainly current in my Jewish-Australian family. One writer pointed out that Dame Mary Gilmore, in *Old Days, Old Ways*, 'describes watching, as a child, her uncle making wooden pegs with which to hobble horses. This was in Wagga Wagga last century. "What's that Uncle Harry?" "A wim wam for a goose's bridle!"' Uncle Harry, as this woman pointed out, was an Ulsterman. Another woman, aged eighty-five was the daughter of an engineer born in England in 1853. Her father had an elaborate workshop 'much frequented by his children'. When they pestered him with 'What is that?' he would reply 'A wing wong for a goose's bridle or a crutch for a duck.'

As the letters mounted up it began to seem that elderly informants whose family memories go directly back, through parents and grandparents, to the mid-nineteenth century, tended to favour 'wing wong' or 'whim wham' rather than 'wig-wam'. But the usage preferred is by no means firmly tied to age. I have asked many people of all ages, both in the Sydney area and in Rockhampton, central Queensland, which word they favour, or think correct. The result of this very unscientific experiment is about 70-30 in favour of 'wigwam'.

So much for the mysterious decoration, or ephemeral piece of finery. But what of the bridle? It had never occurred to me that this word, too, was capable of other interpretations until a woman wrote from a Sydney suburb:

This expression was very commonly used in our family. It was used in the context of 'ask a silly question etc.' or else when they couldn't be bothered explaining what they were doing. For example, 'What are you making?' 'A wim wam for a goose's bridle — to put on a gander's foot.'

The final phrase makes me wonder whether the word was 'bridle' or 'bridal' as a gander is far more likely to be involved in the latter.

When I read that letter the 'pennies dropped'. Subsequently, when I asked people about the phrase I enquired what they understood by bridle/bridal and to my surprise a small but significant number of Australians have always thought of a wedding when they heard the expression.

And this is where I have to leave the puzzle. Perhaps the phrase originated in Elizabethan times and arose from some tale or joke about trumpery finery for the wedding of a strumpet. If anyone knows of such a tale or anecdote or has any further information I should be very interested to hear it.

7

Growing up

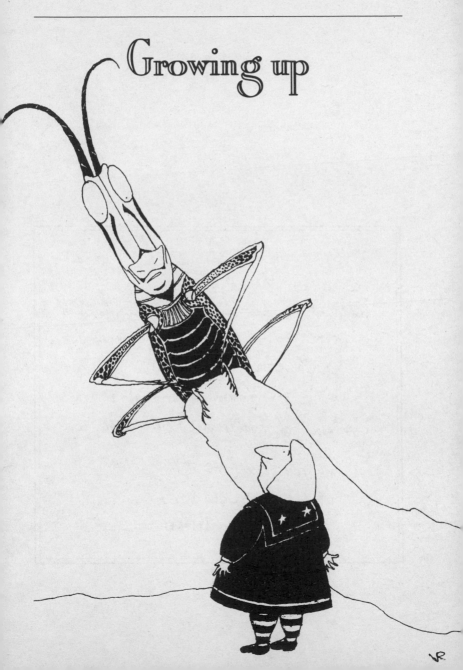

TAKING A SICKIE

Kiddilywinks knee-high to a grasshopper

Going to see the man with the velvet nose

Up before sparrow fart

'WERE YOU BORN IN A TENT?'

A flock of koalas just flew over

MUTTON DRESSED AS SPRING LAMB

A hubcap biter

Linen lifters

In Australia's tropical north there is almost no winter, though nights may be chilly for a few weeks. Further south, the island of Tasmania and some mainland southern highland areas have longer, colder winters but the season is short, and by comparison with much of the Northern Hemisphere, spring is shorter.

Nevertheless, winter is when countless Australians suffer from 'a bit of a sniffle'. Any cold worse than that tends, wrongly, to be called 'flu. Real 'flu is unmistakable; it puts its victims to bed and causes a few days 'off work', taking 'a sickie'.* (Paid sick leave.) Children are amused by 'I opened the door and in flew Enza.'

Year round in city and country Australians spend much of their spare time outdoors. A front porch or verandah is called a patio by owners who wish to sound up with the times, and newer or renovated houses have a paved apron that really is a patio which Australians frequently mispronounce as 'pātio' to rhyme with 'ratio'. The traditional Australian dream is to own a home with a garden which is called a 'yard', but nowadays

---

*'Dog's disease' to some people means 'flu, to others gastro-enteritis.

'units' are popular, home units being what the Americans call 'condominiums'.

Most yards have a 'barbie', this being one of Australia's often remarked upon abbreviations — why most of these end with the suffix 'ie' is unclear. The barbecue may be elaborate and permanent or merely a few loose bricks with a wire grid atop them. Portable barbecues fired by gas cylinders, charcoal or briquettes are in wide use. They fit conveniently in the 'boot' of the family car which may tow a trailer fitted out to accommodate the family motorboat or 'runabout', or, in equestrian families, a horse 'float'.

Despite the proximity of most Australian cities to beautiful beaches and bays, air travellers over many suburbs stare down at unwinking oblong blue eyes, and it often looks as if every house has a backyard swimming pool. As pools proliferate so do backyard drowning tragedies, and prudent parents have their offspring taught to swim at as early an age as possible — nine months is not uncommon. I have heard it said of a jockey who rode a couple of 'duds', 'Arrrr, if he can't swim better than he can ride, one of these days he'll drown in his pool!'

Riding 'trail-bikes', which are small motorised bicycles, is an increasingly popular pursuit. Trail-bike clubs hold races and some of these cater for children of five and six. They use protective safety helmets (known to adult motor-bike riders as 'brain-buckets'), and often this headgear looks larger than the child wearing it.

Country children learn early to avoid 'snakey' places in summer, and other hazards. In bush and suburbs an occasional nesting magpie 'turns really nasty'. Kids with red or fair hair seem to be more at risk from 'dive bombing maggies' than those with darker colouring.

Perhaps because youngsters have to learn self-reliance early, Australian babyhood seems nearly as brief as the spring. This may be why our domestic speech is somewhat 'light on' terms of endearment for infants: one moment a 'bubba' or 'ankle biter' the next a 'littlie', 'kidalidaloo' or 'kiddilywinks', and then, bang, a 'kid'. Once a 'tin lid' (kid), though still 'knee-high to a grass-

'I'll hang you on the wall
for a picture'

hopper' is old enough for exposure to full blasts of family sarcasm, disparagement and home truth that may well not 'let up' until adulthood. In 1908 a Scottish migrant grandmother was saying to an over-tearful boy of four, 'Your eyes are too close to your bladder, dinna greet.' Now the eyes are still too close to bladders, but the advice is 'don't cry/howl/blub'. When the same boy argued he was advised to 'save your breath to cool your porridge', a phrase which is still in use. Many an Australian 'Nana' suspects her chatterbox grandchildren have been 'vaccinated with a gramophone needle'; bless them they would 'argue the leg off an iron pot'. When family loquacity and argument becomes intolerable there is a range of exasperated objection: 'Shut up', 'Let's hear it for a bit of shush', 'I'll hang you on the wall for a picture', 'I'll spiflicate you'.

One woman is recorded as telling her quarrelsome brood, 'You should all have been smothered at birth, not mothered.' Indeed a good deal of Familyspeak sounds cruel, yet it is recollected and reported with affection, amusement and reminiscent pride. I do not think there is any paradox here — what look like blows are no more than gentle cuffs when there is love behind the sarcasm, snub or home truth. One of the people who has helped me with material for this book is a highly qualified social worker, herself a mother of two small children. She works in a home for disadvantaged and/or delinquent children, and has noticed that these deprived and often neglected youngsters have poor vocabularies generally and especially in the range of domestic colloquial speech. Because through speech and in other ways they have not learned, within a loving family circle, to come to terms with ordinary teasing and criticism, they have failed to acquire that useful second skin that prevents us, as we mature, from being unduly 'thin skinned'. They are subject to temper tantrums, which they call 'chucks', at an age when well-adjusted children have learned to cope with, and master, everyday irritation. These children attend an ordinary primary school in the institution's neighbourhood. Many parents of other children at the school are friendly and co-operative. They encourage friendships between their own children and the 'govos' or 'gubbos' as the state wards call themselves, and invite them home after school and at weekends. But these well-intentioned 'ordinary' families experience real difficulty in making the govos feel genuinely accepted, and one of the worst barriers, which also takes longest to overcome, is poverty of language, even for the most usual and basic of household contents, routines and conversation.*

---

*Other words recorded for this group are: sucko (term of abuse and/or provocation — 'tough for you'); chuck (temper tantrum); govo or gubbo (state ward, anything belonging to the government); civo (non-govo); gubbos (secondarily, boiled lollies which come in large tins under government contract); dick, dickhead (a twit); stare off (stop looking at me); talk off (shut up); beako or decko (come and look at this, or stop staring); snako (a crawler, or crawling to an adult); chuck pills (any medication for behaviour); butcher (dentist or barber); to taxi (to hurry and, in the process, do a sloppy job); a scrape (an abortion); to have it off (intercourse). From Anne Stowar, Social Worker, Dept of Youth and Community Services.

More fortunate children experience a sufficiency of necessary love and, in its warmth, learn to behave acceptably and to respect the rights of other family members, old and young. One woman of eighty-four, from an inner-city suburb of Sydney, wrote and gave me several examples of phrases that were used by her mother.

We sure had a lovely young life we only had Mum and she was 29 when Dad died but she was so wonderful. I have lived in [this suburb] 84 years, born here. Mum was so wonderful. I do hope you don't think ... [the phrases she used] are rude but ... [hearing you on radio] sure brought me back to my childhood which was so wonderful.

One of the quoted expressions was 'where there's a will there's a way': that struggling young mother of nearly a century ago certainly made her way to a testimony of which any woman would be proud.

'Children should be seen and not heard' remains in common use but nowadays is understood as a joke rather than an ideal. Equally durable is 'two wrongs don't make a right'. The mean little bird that bedevilled generations continues to chirp to adults what children supposed were close-guarded secrets. Adults who do not wish to tell their age still fob off enquiries with 'I'm as old as my tongue and a little older than my teeth'. Grandparents who tire of strenuous games puzzle with 'I can't, I have a bone in my knee'. Someone who is asked 'Where are you going?' may answer with the widespread 'To see a man about a dog' or the less common, 'To see the man with the velvet nose'.

My maternal grandmother used to break up quarrels by saying 'Birds in their little nests agree.' My sister and I happened to know from direct observation of competitive chicks in nearby trees that this was debatable, but until we settled down granny would not let us intone, in unison with her, the rest of our perennial favourite:

Birds in their little nests agree
It is a sorry sight

81

> When children of one fam-il-eeeee
> Fall out, and chide, and fight.

'Why? Why? Why?' ask the children and are told that 'Y is a crooked letter and will never run straight' or 'Y's a crooked letter and Z's no better' or 'Ask no questions and you'll be told no lies'.

A scowling child with a grievance has 'a face like a twopenny grub', and if it continues to sulk may be warned 'I can see the devil sitting on your shoulder'.

'To be up before sparrow fart' is a virtue. To be lazy, a dawdler or a constant avoider of family tasks and chores is not. 'Who do you think you are? The Lord of the Manor? Get to work'; or 'Who do you think you are? Lord Muck of Turd Island?' or 'What do you think this is? Pineapple Sunday?' Some lazy-bones, who compound their sins by being cheeky, when asked 'What do you think this is? Bush Week?' will answer back, 'Yes, and you're the sap!' They invite such reproofs as 'Watch out else you'll trip over your lip', 'I'll pull your wheels off', or 'Lie down, you're not registered' (which can also be said to chatterboxes and 'skites'). ('Blatherskites' are quite beyond the pale.) When cheek persists, more old fashioned adults may still threaten a taste of 'Paddy-whack-the-drumstick'.

'Now listen here,' exclaims a Sydney mother tried beyond endurance, 'I don't care whether you just jumped off the Harbour Bridge, it's still no excuse.' To an 'uppity' daughter she adds, 'and you'll come down a peg or two Lady Jane!' 'The rainbow after the storm' appears just as the last of the washing up is finished.

'I can see the devil sitting on your shoulder'

A 'slowcoach' will 'meet yourself coming back' and someone delaying the dreaded hour for going to bed 'will meet yourself getting up'.

An indecisive person is advised, 'Either piss or get off the pot.'

A 'fresh air fiend' cannot understand the fondness of others for a nice warm fug, but heartily exclaiming that 'this room is like the Hawkesbury tunnel' throws open doors and windows, thereby perpetuating the days when many a dad smoked shag or plug and steam trains burned coal. Careless folk enter rooms and leave doors open, causing uncomfortable draughts. Perhaps since gold rush days they have been asked 'Born in a tent, eh?' Other inconsiderate souls, often woodworking 'freaks', produce loud banging noises when everyone else is trying to watch 'the box'; to them the sarcastic suggestion is 'drop the other one and we'll all get some sleep'. This quite common expression mystified one child 'since we had no upstairs, or boarder who dropped his boots, this one was a puzzle at the time'.

In a strict Methodist household a young woman hurriedly stitched up a laddered stocking one Sunday morning. 'You'll have to unpick every one of those stitches with your nose when you get to heaven,' warned her mother. A ladder in a stocking is known as 'a stairway to heaven'.

Had Christopher Robin been an Australian child the answer to his plaintive query, 'Has anybody seen my mouse?' might have been 'It's up in Annie's room behind the clock.'* Variants of this widespread saying are 'Up in Annie's room resting on a pedestal' or 'hanging on a cobweb'.

We all, at some time, have searched vainly for an object that is plainly visible to everyone else. In such instances the derisive advice might be 'If it was a dog it would bite you'; 'follow your

---

*A Sydney man tells me his grandfather used to hide important documents such as house deeds and sometimes paper money behind the face of a clock. A watchmaker tells me old-fashioned chiming mantel clocks have space often utilised in this way. Their outer cases leave considerable free space inside.

nose, it's a steep hill' and 'you couldn't see a bull through a hole in the fence'.

Sometimes a worm will attempt to turn and protests at kindly banter, but protest merely invites a further flood of home truths, concluding with 'so stick that up your jumper' or 'put that in your pipe and smoke it'. 'Got a match?' 'If I had one for you I'd start a travelling circus.' 'Arrrr, pull y' head in!' 'If I had a face like yours I would!' 'The softest part of you is your teeth!'

Little children frequently mis-hear or misunderstand events in the surrounding world. When one is 'knee high to a grass-hopper' one's viewpoint is closer to the ground than that of fully grown people. To someone less than a metre tall the crowd of shoppers that mum rather enjoys can be a tiresome, and even alarming vision of a procession of articulated legs and knees.

Years ago a Sydney newspaper carried a story of a young woman, *not* a 'Holy Roman', who entered a crowded tram bur-dened with parcels and a couple of weary, whining (or 'whing-ing') toddlers. A man stood up for her, and she took the youngest child on her knee while one of two nuns sitting together across the aisle lifted the older one onto her lap. In those days nuns wore black habits and veils with white wimples surrounding their faces and white starched collars. The little girl was shy and for a while alarmed, but the sisters put her at ease and were soon having an animated conversation with the child. When the mother was ready to leave the tram and collected her daughter one of the nuns said, 'Please don't disillusion her. She thinks we're penguins!'

Many children's incredible stories and statements are of the innocent penguin order, and affectionate families understand this. All the same, as youngsters grow from babyhood it is important that they learn to distinguish harmless fibbing and misapprehension from deliberate falsehood. Thoroughly im-probable accounts, or the deliberate lies of older children may be greeted by 'Like wax!', 'Tell *that* to the marines', 'Oh yeah!

And there's a horse in the bathroom!', 'Pull the other one [leg] it plays jinglebells!', 'Oh yeah, *and* a flock of koalas just flew over'* or 'Yes, and a chicken has lips'.

'All my eye and Betty Martin', one long-lived expression in this category, came to Australia like much other colloquialism from Britain and has been common 'since Adam was a pup', or 'since Jesus Christ played full-back for Jerusalem'. An elderly correspondent gave me a slight variant and writes that her mother,

when the children were trying to 'put one over her' and she knew it was a fib would say, 'That's all my eye and Biddy Martin'. I've often wondered about 'Biddy Martin', an old Englishwoman apparently in the village who was famous for not very carefully following the truth … I'm sure no one would have heard it in these modern times.

But she would be surprised; several other people report it but of Betty not Biddy.

---

*The flock of koalas is a central Queensland usage that seems to bear some relationship to the 'drop bears' of Gladstone, central Queensland. The 'drop bears' are creatures of a tall story — they were invented during World War II for the benefit of gullible American servicemen. It is alleged that 'drop bears' are a dangerous kind of koala and that they drop out of trees on the heads and shoulders of bush walkers and hug them to death.

A hardened liar will attempt to 'look as innocent as a cat in a goldfish bowl' but as a rule older people can 'see the wheels going round in your head'. You can't fool mum who, as if by magic, can always tell whose 'sticky fingers' have been into the biscuit container.

Half-deafened mums complain that over-talkative children (or for that matter, adults) give them 'corns on the ears' and may exclaim, 'Leave off! Leave off!' or 'Oh, fiddle de dee!' There is a withering snub to those who butt into conversations, often with irrelevant information or useless advice: 'I was talking to the butcher, not the block!' or 'to the maggot, not the meat'. 'She could talk a glass eye to sleep!'

The handwriting of the following letter suggests that its writer is elderly; she was one of nine children and when they exasperated their mother 'which was often, she would chase us, exclaiming "I will kill you, as sure as God made little apples." Every time I see little apples, they stir up memories.'

Mock threats like this, when affection underlies them, do not leave scars. Women whose little children are perpetually under foot, or whose older ones hang about the kitchen when mum is trying to prepare a meal, are understood to be joking behind their annoyance when they threaten to 'sweep you out with the tea leaves', a phrase that recalls an era before vacuum cleaners, or even, perhaps, 'box brooms' (carpet sweepers). Used tea leaves were emptied from pot to bucket and later strewn, damp, on floors and carpets where they collected dust and were easily seen while sweeping.

And to order children out of the kitchen: 'Kid you're a tap and run!'; 'kid you're an egg and beat it!'; 'kid you're a nut and bolt!'. 'Make like a tree, and leave!'; 'make like a bee and buzz!' What is more, 'get moving quick sticks' or 'licketty split'.

Fashion is an unending source of family fun. Older women may be criticised for dressing unsuitably and pretending to be 'mutton dressed as spring lamb', but at least this kind of disparaging remark is usually made behind the offender's back. Few families display such tact — or hypocrisy — when a youngster's taste in clothes comes into question. Young people who 'dress to kill', or 'dress up like a sore thumb' or 'the cat's meow'* are fair game for domestic wits. As if by some mysterious natural law, the new fashions and styles adopted by every generation are bound to seem 'way out', utterly ridiculous, even positively objectionable and dangerous to their seniors. My father couldn't understand why his daughters wanted to 'put all that muck on your faces', and my aunt and mother (backed up by occasional pontifications from the medical profession) prophesied orthopaedic doom when we tottered on high heels or even the relatively stable 'platforms' that were 'in' during World War II. Collective memory is short. Today many girls eschew powder, lipstick and foundation lotion, concentrating all their cosmetics on their eyes; older people think they look 'insipid and like zombies' while others say they resemble 'Egyptian tarts'.

There is, 'to coin a phrase', nothing new under the sun. Governor Bligh's daughter, Mrs Mary Putland, in 1807 wore a new-fangled dress to church, and the rude convicts, who were compulsorily mustered to attend divine worship (Anglican), laughed so heartily she fainted. This occurrence added one more straw of grievance to her irascible father's tally of dislike for a colony whose leading citizens were soon to depose him. Mary's costume would have been the loose-fitting empire-style and have displayed a generous expanse of bosom, which she may have covered with a gauzy fichu. Presumably, for church going, she would have worn long lace-trimmed pantaloons underneath her muslin skirt, especially in a backward colony like New South Wales where to show legs through transparent material may have been impossibly 'fast'. Mrs Putland's fashionable young contemporaries in Europe just then went virtually 'topless' to evening routs and balls and some damped their transparent gowns so that they clung revealingly over precious little underwear.

---

*They can also be 'dressed up like a sore toe' or 'dressed to the nines'.

The Regency generation of middle and upper class young girls lived to share, with their daughters and granddaughters, adoption of the crinoline, but, though legs were then coyly hidden by wire hoops and layers of petticoat, fashionable evening gowns continued to reveal expanses of shoulder and bosom despite the fulminations of early equivalents of 'The Festival of Light'. Yet, by the 1930s, when 'backless dresses' and 'lounging pyjamas', which were in a way resurrections of the pantaloon, were introduced, the female top had long been well covered, and women had forgotten the feel of trouser-like garments. During the flaming twenties the bust bodice, and early forms of brassiere, or bra, flattened breasts to the desirable contour of a laundry scrubbing board. So backless dresses and swimming 'cossies' with halter necks were frowned upon as utterly indecent when they were introduced. By then, skirts which had been worn above the knee by 1920s 'flappers' were quite long again. Yet grandmothers of the 'mini-skirt' era who had themselves lived through those earlier controversies 'carried on a treat' as if never before had so much leg been seen. Inconsistently, when the mini-skirt generation switched to long 'hippie' dresses and skirts, or uni-sex and exceedingly cover-up jeans, the protest renewed. The young can't win, in one way, but in another they always do.

In fashion matters young men must also endure family derision. In the affluent 1960s 'teenagers' became a valuable market for the rag trade, so the 'chiacking' and chorus of disapproval began earlier, continued longer, and reached its crescendo when youths aspired to grow their hair to shoulder length and sprout beards as soon as they were able. For some extraordinary reason this trend was often considered very decadent indeed. Yet many of the adults who grumbled and fulminated loudest and most vehemently were proud of the family album in which pioneer great grandfather posed with his resplendent 'ziff' often reaching to the level of his floral or patterned waistcoat with its fancy buttons. The larrikins and larrikinesses of the 1890s and early 1900s, who favoured their era's 'way out' gear, must also have left descendants. But to listen to a present day family chorus, augmented by school principals, newspaper leader-writers and correspondents to their letter columns, one might be pardoned for supposing that never, until the mid-twentieth century, had the human male in western societies displayed his physical charms.

A fly on the wall of the 'lounge' (sitting room/parlour) observes Karen, who has just started work as a 'steno-sec' or hospital 'pro' or 'schoolie' or cadet 'journo'. Karen has donned her 'glad rags' for a 'date'. Her aunts and grandmothers, like their elders before them peer from the 'easy chairs' and sofa of the 'lounge suite' and complain that her wage packet goes 'straight onto her back'. Where is she off to? To a disco, with Terry.

Chorus: 'Don't mix with scrowchers'; 'Remember what the girl did' and, grudgingly, 'Well, you look good enough for the man you're after'. There is no suggestion that Karen is a 'hubcap biter' (girls who chase boys because of their cars). Grannie cautions against 'linen lifters' and 'pirates', mum against 'wolves'. One acidulous aunt is heard to mutter that flighty girls 'should all be dressed in tin pants and the openers hidden'.

Karen's troubles! Having privately consulted the medical staff of a women's medical centre she has decided not to risk being 'on the pill'. Who wants a 'clot'? She's 'on the loop', and good luck to her.

8

Linda!
Ecology begins at home

HAIR LIKE A BIRCH BROOM IN A FIT

Skinny as a walking hairpin

Living on the smell of an oily rag

You can't tell a book by its cover

TIGHT AS A FISH'S BUM AND THAT'S
WATER TIGHT

Skin a louse for its hide

Rooms that resemble 'a fowl-yard on Christmas Day with all the chooks drunk' or 'a Chinese brothel on Sunday morning' are a perennial source of domestic friction. Some of the scathing phrases they give rise to are interchangeable with expressions used to describe 'scungy'-looking people, so that both a girl and her bedroom may resemble 'a dog's dinner'.

Perennial, too, is the warfare waged between houseproud mums and their grubby brats. These conflicts are bases for much enjoyable literature as witness the seemingly immortal popularity of Norman Lindsay's *Saturdee*. No Australian before or since Lindsay has better described the antagonisms generated between, in the one camp, ma, aunts and 'uppity' sisters and, in the other, boys of an age that prefers, and truthfully seldom perceives, grime.

No doubt, even in bygone times, girls were also offenders — they certainly are today. When in the 1960s schoolchildren became obsessed with conservation and ecology issues, one exasperated Australian mother cut a cartoon from the *New Yorker* and pasted it to her daughter's bedroom door. (To the credit of that thirteen-year-old-girl, she accepted and shared the

93

joke at the expense of a sanctum that habitually looked as if 'it had been stirred with a stick'.) Between the pictured American bedroom and its Australian counterpart there was an uncanny resemblance: the unmade bed a repository for tennis racquet and guitar; shoes, socks, papers and 'undies' all over the floor; chair strewn with coats, a rug, a 'tote bag'; desk like the layers of ancient Troy; pictures and posters askew on the walls. The American teenager stood in the midst of the confusion, her hair like 'a birchbroom [or golliwog] in a fit' when her harassed mother appeared at the doorway and exclaimed 'Linda, Ecology begins at home!'

Looking 'like a wild man from Borneo', especially if he's been playing 'footie' on a muddy field, many a lad comes home, or many a lass sandy and sunburnt from the beach, to be greeted by: 'You look like something the cat dragged in and the dog didn't want', or you look 'as if you'd been dragged through a hedge [or mangle] backwards'. Mangles, long superseded, are immortalised in current Familyspeak.

By this time of late afternoon the house has been furbished 'within an inch of its life' and is 'clean as a whistle' or 'a new pin'. It would be a brave spider who would dare weave 'Irish curtains' across its windows and a foolhardy 'wog' or 'bug' or 'creepy crawly' that braved its insecticided cupboards.

It is high summer. Cicadas, popularly called 'locusts', which they are not — locusts are grasshoppers popularly called 'hoppers'

. . . something the cat dragged in . . .

94

Cocky

— drum insistently from garden trees. Because it is daylight saving time an Australian suburban family plans to enjoy its Friday evening meal 'up the yard' using the outdoor tables and chairs near the 'barbie'. Everyone helps to carry out the food and some wit cries, 'And don't forget!' this being an advertising slogan which has really 'caught on' for a brand of insect repellent. Dad, 'old fuddy-duddy' (or sceptic) has also lit a mosquito coil against 'mossies', 'sandies' (sand flies) and other 'bities'.

Kid brother slams down a pile of plates and rushes over to the lemon tree where he swoops on an evening-sluggish 'greengrocer'. His tally for today (which he keeps in a shoe box — his elders protest this practice is cruel but do nothing to stop him) has been two 'greengrocers', a 'black prince' and one 'yellow Monday '. His ambition is to capture a rare 'cherry nose' or an even rarer 'floury baker'. It is a bumper year for cicadas.

A raucous flock of 'cockies' flashes overhead; must be the drought that's sending the 'rainbows' (rainbow lorikeets) this close to the coast. A watchful 'maggie' perches on the fence, a 'kooka' on the clothes hoist and a peewit pecks the lawn almost underfoot. Greedy suburban birds grow very tame, and their claws are impervious to 'bindis' (bindi-i is a burr that grows in grass).

After 'tea', which is dinner, the younger kids 'hop' or 'whip' indoors to watch telly but the 'rest of the mob' pours itself

95

another glass all round from the 'cask', which is a plastic skin holding wine and fitted with a plastic tap. Then mum, dad and elder sister and brother settle themselves for an enjoyable 'chinwag' — for once the whole family has a night at home.

The past working week is in review. Mother 'whipped up' to the shops for weekend provisions this morning and was 'put out' because that 'jumped up' young woman from the new house 'down the road', a real 'parve' (*parvenue*) or 'Johnny come lately', 'butted in' and got served out of turn by the 'skirt happy' butcher's offsider. Dad says mum's a bit hard on the newcomer. Why 'have a down' on her? He had 'a bit of a chat' with her last week at the newsagent's and she's not 'a bad sort'. This response makes mum huffy. 'Just because she's "as skinny as a walking hairpin" or skinny as a "gas pipe cut on the bias" or "a matchstick with all the wood shaved off", you think she's "the ants pants".' Mum's approaching 'her change' and fears that, like her own mother before her, she may 'lose her figure' and end up 'built like a battleship'. Moreover, she's convinced the offending young woman is 'a proper little piece' — young and all as she is, her present husband is her 'second lump of sugar'.

Elder sister, too, is envious of the tall, thin 'trendy' neighbour. She supports mum: 'If that girl drank a glass of tomato juice you could use her for a thermometer.'

'Puss puss, meow meow,' jeers elder brother.

'Then,' mum continues, 'I "ran into" dear old Mrs Jones.'

'*That* old tabbie!' dad snorts, his womenfolk have aggrieved him. 'That old perambulating ragbag!'

'Oh, she's really not a bad old girl,' mum says mildly. 'She lives on "the smell of an oiled rag", and really I don't know how pensioners manage with inflation so bad. They can't have "two sixpences to jingle on a tombstone". She bought a pound of "boneless"* but she doesn't keep a pet, so you know what *that* means.

---

*'Boneless' is boneless beef, scraps and offcuts that are fit for human consumption, but sold cheaply as pet food. Butchers are not allowed, by law, to label these scraps as 'pet food'. Some butchers also label bones for dogs 'woofer bones'.

'fiddle the till'

I'd hate to have to wait for "the day the eagle shits" (pension day) so I could afford something tasty to eat.'

They agree that the butcher charges 'like a wounded billy-goat' or 'a mad bull'.

Now it is 'on for young and old'. Sister had 'a go in' with her arch enemy from Accounts, the one with 'a face like the back of a tram smash' and a 'nit picker' of note.

Dad says 'you can't tell a book by its cover', and he'd prefer sister's *bête noir* to a 'smoothie' any day. He recalls a ledger-keeper at his 'place' (of work) who 'fiddled the till' and 'lined his own pocket' yet who had a face 'nice and open, like a jam tin', which was an invaluable asset for a 'con artist'. This 'crim' 'diddled' Dad's firm for years before the 'white collar fuzz' (police anti-fraud squad) were set on his trail. But the embezzler 'got wind' of the investigation, 'jumped before he was pushed', 'shot through like a Bondi tram' and is now believed to be 'living it up' overseas.

Few would seriously dispute a person's right to 'put a bit of fruit on the sideboard' by taking advantage of 'perks' considered legitimate. The dividing line between what is allowed and what is excessive can be hard to define, but no honest person would dream of 'snitching' money, or stamps, or a typewriter. To take pencils, writing blocks and paper clips is OK; to carry home an unopened carton of envelopes would be stealing. All the same, petty pilfering (and unauthorised STD calls) are a worrying hidden cost to many businesses — and no stolen phone call ever 'fell off the back of a truck' or 'off the end of the wharf'.

Brother takes his turn for a hearty grumble about *his* boss who admittedly has 'a face like the north end of a south-bound bus' but is really a good sport who only occasionally 'gets on brother's wick'.

This is sensitive ground because brother's employer is a politician who belongs to a party that dad despises; the family is not at one politically and tries to avoid the topic. So the conversation lapses awaiting a tactful change of direction and, meanwhile, sister replenishes the glasses. 'I don't mind if I do,' says mum when asked if she'd like 'a drop' more, and meaning 'of course'.

Mum says, 'Dad, if you'd rather have a beer there's a couple of nice cold "arrises" in the fridge.' ('Arris' is a bottle, and rhymes with Aristotle.)

But dad prefers to 'stick with the plonk'.* He and mum smile fondly at each other. Good humour is restored. And it is dad who 'hits on' the entrancing topic that never fails to unite all self-respecting Ockers. This evening it arose during the follow-

---

*One explanation for this word was that during World War I Australian soldiers in France mispronounced *vin blanc* as 'plonk'. In his *Dictionary of Rhyming Slang* (2nd edition, 1961) Julian Franklyn lists 'plink plonk' as slang for *vin blanc*.

ing exchange: sister, when she turned on the wine-tap over dad's glass in the gathering darkness of that still-warm evening, overfilled it, just to the brim.

'If you can drink that without spilling any it proves you're not jealous,' laughs mum and, she mock-chides her daughter, 'You'll have to do better than that or you'll never be married'. (A woman who can judge accurately the exact capacity of a container is sure to be a spinster. Nevertheless, mum is a whizz at selecting the precise size of basin that will accommodate the brew of soup to be poured from a saucepan.)

'Sorry,' says sister, 'my hand slipped.'

Dad takes his glass, sips, doesn't spill a drop and says to his daughter, 'Well, at least you weren't stingy.'

Thus is uttered the name of the Number One Deadly Sin: Meanness. The worst thing any Australian woman, man or child can be is mean.

A race against time begins, and for this reason mum, if 'she gets her head' would carry on till 'sparrow fart' about a certain farmer on the north coast of New South Wales where she, the daughter of a farmer, was born and raised. The other members of her family hope to 'head her off' from these oft-told tales.

That neighbour of mum's youth, though very prosperous, was notoriously mean. 'Tight as a fish's bum, and that's tight', or 'tight as a fish's arse and that's water tight.' It was commonly said of him that 'he fed his family on cracked corn and redbill soup', the redbill being a native swamp hen, common in that region but regarded as virtually useless tucker. Such unappetising fare apart, his meal-table was rumoured to be 'as bare as a badger's bum'. In those days people were less self conscious about racist remarks than is now the case, and mum's mother intended no actual prejudice or offence when she referred to her mean neighbour as a real 'ikey mo', 'mean as Moses' or, even-handedly, 'stingy as a Scotchman'.

Dad manages to 'get his oar in' ahead of mum by recalling his Uncle Cec, notoriously 'too tight to pass a raspberry seed', who always offered remarkable excuses for failure to produce small change when 'the hat was sent round' for some good cause or other. Cec was alleged 'to have a scorpion [or death adder] in his pocket'.

Sister thinks being parsimonious with money is bad enough, but the kind of person who is even worse 'wouldn't show his blind old aunt a short cut out to the dunny', or 'lend you the harness off his nightmare', or 'give you the sleeves out of his vest'. (A vest being a singlet that has no sleeves.)

'Sheilas can be just as miserable,' brother cuts in. 'That "old chook" up the corner shop 'd "skin a louse for its hide".'

'*Or* "pinch a lick" of a kid's all day sucker,' laughs sister.

'My goodness! Kids!' exclaims mother. 'It's far past their bedtime. They'll meet themselves getting up!' She rushes into the house and switches off the television set in the midst of a sex and violence movie which her younger children have been watching with unaccustomed and uninterrupted enjoyment. The family's inevitable agreeable discussion on a second deadly sin, Laziness, must await another occasion. The 'mozzie coil' is just about burned to powdery ash. Dad and his elder children carry used utensils and the last of the cask indoors. Before he leaves the yard dad scrapes the limp remains of a salad into the compost bin. Waste not, want not.* Charity, in its widest sense, may not be evident in this home, but ecology begins there.

---

*To be recited in a mock parsonical voice:
> Dearly beloved brethren
> Is it not a sin
> When you peel potatoes
> To throw away the skin?
> For the skin feeds the pigs
> And the pigs feed you
> Dearly beloved brethren
> Is not this true?
>   (woman, born Melbourne circa 1850)

9

Akubras, shirts and Vegemite and mums and other things

NO WOCKING FURRIES

Water wings

Seasoned Globites

Squashed ants and worms

TOE JAM

Nobody loves me, everybody hates me
Think I'll go eat worms!
Big ones, small ones
Fat ones, thin ones
Worms that squiggle and squirm.

Bite their heads off
Suck their blood out
Throw their skins away.
Nobody knows how much I enjoy
Eating worms three times a day!*

The trouble with ready-made clothing these days is that half the garments one buys have been 'stitched with a red hot needle and a burning thread': their seams come adrift and their hems fall down. Buttons, attached by intricate loops of thread resembling very fine fishing line fall off at first wearing. Quite expensive garments prove to be made of material so poor that, after one or two washes, 'you could shoot peas through it'.

All the same, an advantage that clothes off-the-hook will always have over the productions of a home dressmaker, is that one can try them on, see how they look, and avoid the risk of a dress that 'fits all over, touches nowhere'.

An immutable law of clothing is that fashion-conscious persons seldom own exactly the right garments for particular occasions.

'What'll I wear?'

'A pink shirt with purple spots and a white owl's feather' is not the most helpful suggestion. Many people solve their problems by appearing in jeans and T-shirts at every conceivable

---

*A song popular among schoolchildren circa 1960s.

and many an inconceivable event. The lettering of T-shirts could be a study on its own account. NO WOCKING FURRIES announces one. FUZZY DUCK (front) DOES 'E EVER (back) suits males and TRY ME FOR SIZE is unisex. MY MEAN OLD OLDIES WENT ON THIS FABULOUS TRIP TO HAWAII/SINGAPORE/AUCKLAND/PERTH (you name it) AND ALL THEY BROUGHT ME BACK WAS THIS ROTTEN T-SHIRT is universal. Buttons printed with slogans seem to be passé, but car-stickers remain alive and well everywhere: 'If you can read this, thank a teacher'; 'Insanity is infectious — you catch it from your children'; 'Beat Telecom — train a homing pigeon'.

The greatest Australian sartorial revolution of the twentieth century, however, has to do with hats. White Australians and their hats were inseparable from the earliest days of settlement until, during the 1960s, shady headgear was relinquished gradually in cities, and often in the country. Great-grandparents had become adept at fashioning cabbage-tree hats from a local palm; then the Yankee 'Wideawake' took over during the gold rushes. Women wore sunbonnets for everyday and whatever millinery was fashionable for best. Cartoons of larrikinesses (or 'donahs') of the 1890s-1900s period show the hats worn by them and other 'flash' girls in a great variety of exaggerated forms that often look like parodies of more conventional fashions. City people used to reckon they could spot a country family visiting town from a mile off chiefly because of the outline of their hats, whose brims were wide and shapes practical.

Men's felt hats, often known as 'Akubras' after a well-known local brand, were much more stable, as to fashion, than women's models. Gradually, the high-crowned shape of the early twentieth century — dented in the middle and worn straight on the head — yielded to jauntier styles like the pork pie (which often had a small feather angled in its ribbon band).

In the mid 1930s the wilder lads of Sydney Grammar School took to contorting their school-uniform's traditional headgear into a flattened shape as close to a pork pie as it would go, which they wore at a perilous angle over one ear, and the outraged voices of their parents and schoolmasters fulminated about decadence and what were the nation's young coming to. Futile attempts at prevention were attempted. In time, the improvised shape was itself adopted as school uniform — if you can't beat them, join them. When these wild lads' sons, decades later, wished to grow their hair to shoulder length and abandon hats altogether, the historical process was repeated. Inevitably, though not without emotional scars and compulsory barbering, the lads won.

One contributory factor to the decline of the hat industry was myxomatosis, the introduced virus that nation-wide halted, and often virtually eradicated, Australia's endemic plague of rabbits. While the nation rode to prosperity on the sheep's back its face was shaded under a mountain of trapped rabbits whose fur was made into felt.

Countless people, particularly older ones, still wore hats, leading to the cab-drivers' folklore that maintains any ordinary driver wearing one is a disaster area to be overtaken or otherwise escaped from as quickly as possible. Like much folklore this belief contains truthful elements.

Once when Australians went to the beach for a 'dip'* they carried 'cossies', 'bathers' or 'togs', or in South Australia 'swimmies'. Henry Lawson's advice about rolling a swag was adaptable to the sausage achieved by rolling 'cossie', rubber cap and bottle of carron or coconut oil neatly in an old towel whose selvedge edges were firmly turned in over the contents before the whole was tightly rolled from end to end — it fitted snugly under one's arm. Non-swimmers also took 'water wings' (inflatable floats), and we wore large shady hats. Gradually hats were discarded in favour of beach umbrellas, sunglasses and white zinc cream plastered over noses, cheekbones and even, sometimes, the tops of ears — young Australians began to resemble a subculture of clowns.

Altering customs of this order reflected the universal ownership of cars (no one could carry umbrellas and bulging beach

---

*Sidney J. Baker in *The Australian Language* noticed that 'dip' in this sense has sheep-dipping antecedents.

'water wingo'

bags on trams), and increased general affluence that enabled people to buy countless sun creams, lotions and potions rather than one tennis shade or straw hat that would last for several seasons.

During the last few years, however, alarming medical statistics have forced Australians to consider the price paid in skin cancer by its hatless, sleeveless population and by heedless baskers on beaches. Entirely irrespective of high fashion, hats are coming into their own again. In parts of Queensland they are now obligatory for primary-school children who, unlike their parents' generation when young, wear them willingly. The school-uniform hats of today bear little resemblance to the straw 'donkeys' breakfasts' of bygone times; some are floppy, others resemble baseball caps — inverted basins with jutting eye-shade — and all are washable, made from nylon and other light synthetic fabrics.

The revolutionary effect of the nylon age on schoolchildren

is not confined to hats. Years ago synthetic bags (especially favoured are those resembling jet-set issue from airlines) ended the Globite era when every fibre school suitcase (or 'port'* in Queensland and a few other places), whether or not it was a representative of that well-known brand with its globe of the world stamped below the handle, was called 'me Globite'.

Genuine Globites cost more than many other brands; they were status symbols with this qualification: a new Globite was one of the most disgraceful things a child could own. A respectable Globite was richly seasoned without and within. Outside, the owner carved her name into the shiny ridged fibre and filled the intaglio with ink. She banged it along fences to batter it acceptably and sat on it at bus or tram stops, confident its strong hinges and clasps would never yield but that its shape, over all, would assume subtle distortions. It was by its dark brown interior, however, that aficionados judged a vintage Globite. It opened to a warm, rank and indefinable smell that adults avoided whenever possible. Inside the slightly curved lid were messages, stickers, inked names; randomly over the entire inner surface were Rorschach-like legacies of leaking 'Platignums' ('Platignum' was the pre-'biro' generic term for fountain pens) adding to the interest. But it was the smell that dominated all, recalling countless paper-bags of school lunch and 'play lunch'; it was redolent of oranges, squashed pears, tomatoes and tomato sauce, hard-boiled egg, raw onion, 'soap' (processed cheese), cold meats, stale bread, rancid butter and Anzac bickies. And ... Vegemite.

Ah Vegemite! Innocent uninitiates or 'new kids' may have allowed their mums to put Vegemite on sandwiches; some appallingly misguided mums were conned by 'Back to School' suggestions in the cookery pages of women's magazines and experimented with Vegemite and grated cheese, Vegemite and cucumber, Vegemite and chopped walnuts and other 'yucky' and wholly impossible stuff. Their kids soon disabused them of

---

*In Queensland a Millaquin port was a sugar bag, the term deriving from the Millaquin Sugar Mill.

the notion that either mums or nationally-respected cookery editors know the first thing about Vegemite.

There is only one way to eat the beautiful black goo at school; one way, with a minor variation in serving (explained below), that permits a kid to actually enjoy, nay lust after, a food that is full of vitamins, not sweet and — dreaded term — 'good for you'. Vita Wheat biscuits, crunchy rectangles pierced with rows of little holes, and also nutritious, are an essential of the recipe.

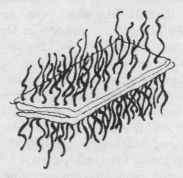

Recipe (for one serving, increase as desired)
Ingredients: Two Vita-Wheat biscuits, butter or substitute, Vegemite.
Method: Spread the biscuits with butter or substitute, and liberally with Vegemite. Sandwich gently together. A light touch is essential at this stage.

Wrap in grease-proof paper and place in paper bag with (optional and according to availability and taste) packet of sandwiches, slice of cake, banana, apple or fruit in season.

Place all in bulging Globite and press firmly against (optional as above) pens, pencils, rubbers, grubby 'nose rag' (handkerchief), sandshoes if sports day, exercise books, text books, library books, 'cardie', packet of sneezing powder.

Those intending to serve 'squashed ants' below, should if possible leave Globite in hot sun all morning. Those preferring 'worms' should leave Globite in a shady place.
To Serve: 'Squashed ants'. Press warm biscuits together firmly. The half-melted thin line of black squiggles that ooze from the holes are 'squashed ants'.

'Worms' or 'wormy biscuits'. As for 'squashed ants' but biscuits should be cooler. The long black threads that issue from the holes — and with this variant practice makes perfect and amazing lengths may be achieved — are 'worms'.

Before relinquishing the topic of worms it should be noted that in the 1930s and 40s when tinned spaghetti in tomato sauce, and tinned baked beans in tomato sauce, were staple fillings for school sandwiches, the playground phrase 'Swap you a beetle for a worm' did not refer to Vegemite.

When children abandoned the time-honoured Globite, an Australian invention, as important in its day as the stump jump plough, vanished into the obscurity of history. The saddest aspect of its passing was that, unwittingly, kids lost one of their staunchest weapons in childhood's immemorial fight to preserve its privacy. No adult would willingly have investigated the mysteries of a vintage Globite.

For no better reason than that it, too, is a topic revolting to all right-thinking adults, I here commemorate 'toe jam'. I first heard of 'toe jam' in central Queensland and am not sure how wide its currency is throughout Australia. The Queensland author and folklorist Bill Scott replied as follows to my somewhat puzzled request for enlightenment:

Toe jam? Of course. Maybe it's a Queensland expression, and certainly I hadn't heard it since my youth, but after wearing shoes and socks to Sunday School (about the only time we did wear them), I remember still the incredible luxury of taking them off on the way home. The dust rose from the unmade road and crept down our woollen socks. When you took off your shoes the ribbed patterns were visible on your skin, and between the toes was a sort of mixture of perspiration and dust. This was luxuriously rubbed out with our fingers, and the resulting little rolls of dirt were certainly called 'toe jam'.

10

If it doesn't fatten it will fill

Snake's bum on a biscuit

But you mustn't curse nor grumble — what won't fatten will fill up

'The Old Bark Hut', old bush song

Rolly, rolly round the table
Fill your belly while you're able

Boys' school grace, circa 1930

Holy Mary, Mother of grace
Hold them back while I wash my face

Boys' school grace, circa 1930

May you live long enough there's no bugger left to bury you

Australian toast

The Lord be praised!
My belly's raised,
For each plateful
We are grateful,
      Heavenly Pa! Ta!

Grace contributed by an old people's social group, Lidcombe, NSW

After spilling salt, throw a pinch over your left shoulder and say: 'May the beggars bite their tongues'.

Superstitious Australian mother, circa 1930*

Q. How long till dinner?
A. In two shakes of a pussycat's foot.

Oh, how the boarders yell
When they hear the dinner bell!

Old song

Q. Grandpa, why do you always go to the dunny when the dinner bell rings?
A. Cos that's the only time all the flies is in the kitchen.

Australian joke

FURTB Full up, ready to bust
QFRTB Quite full, ready to bust

Fingers were made before forks

---

*This same mother 'always made us say "White Rabbits" when she woke us up in the morning on the first day of each month. This was supposed to bring good luck.' According to some correspondents 'White Rabbits' was only said if the month has an 'r' in it.

Australia grows good food and, on the whole, it is cooked well and with imagination. It was not ever thus.

In his book *Triumph of the Nomads* (Macmillan, 1975), Geoffrey Blainey noted that in many parts of the country the diet of white men was once extremely poor, although Aborigines frequently fed extremely well. Many outback workers who drew the nineteenth century ration, known as 'Eight, ten, two, and a quarter' (8lb flour, 10lb meat, 2lb sugar, ¼lb tea) suffered from deficiency diseases under a host of local and popular names, though good bushmen who were prepared to experiment with 'bush tucker', or acquired knowledge of edible plants and fruits, often kept healthy.

Some present day mining operations in remote areas are successful in places near, or akin to, those where nineteenth century attempts to develop gold deposits failed.* The failures were chiefly due to high death rates of miners, and, significantly, these were caused by bad and inadequate food and temperature extremes. Not only mechanical scoops and draglines, but

---

The Northern Territory and its Goldfields, George M. Newman, Adelaide, 1875.

also air-conditioning, refrigeration and air-lifted frozen food make possible today's mineral booms.

During and after World War II, for some reason or reasons, Australians quite suddenly became willing, indeed eager, to experiment with the cuisines of other countries. This phenomenon has been attributed to large migrations of people from Europe and Asia, but that explanation seems over-simple to me. I suspect that the presence in this country of large numbers of US and other troops during the war, increasing affluence in the population and even better school education had something to do with the change. Generations of Australians who preferred steak and eggs to anything else (with a garnish of shredded lettuce and pickled beetroot, the whole smothered under tomato and/or worcestershire sauce) *could* have eaten more adventurously, and even more cheaply, either in their own homes or in cafés. Those Greek families who traditionally cooked the steak and eggs in countless country town cafés, known as 'th'

Greeks', were responding to an invariable, or nearly invariable, demand.

My friend Bob C. was a commercial traveller in New South Wales during the 1930s. He journeyed by train in those days when every sizeable country town had at least one hotel, usually called the Commercial Hotel or the Railway Hotel, that provided a 'Travellers Room'. Nowadays, travellers carry their samples in their cars or station wagons and visit shop-keepers. In Bob's time, shop-keepers visited the traveller in the Travellers Room, and ordered from wares displayed on its tables.

When Bob C. arrived in a town by the morning train he booked himself and his suitcases full of samples into the appropriate hostelry, left his bags unpacked and immediately looked for the Greek café. 'Now,' he'd say to the proprietor, 'I'll be here for tonight' (or two nights in larger centres) 'and I'd like to eat in your café. BUT I DON'T WANT STEAK AND EGGS. If you and your wife don't mind I'd like a serving of whatever you and your family are having for your own meal. Just put in extra food for me, and I'll pay whatever you think is fair for whatever it is. No, I've no time for a discussion. I like Greek food and I eat everything.'

Bob dined magnificently all over New South Wales and seldom at a café table, either. He was usually invited to the family dwelling behind, or nearby, or above the café and made an honoured guest at a banquet that, with immense pleasure, his new friends had worked most of the day to prepare. Bob would arrive bearing a bottle or two of wine purchased, according to his story, after the licensee of the Commercial or Railway had recovered from the shock of a respectable gent in hardware asking for 'plonk'; then a small stock of good wine (sometimes superb wine) was unearthed from forgotten recesses at the back of the bar.

But the gastronomic pleasures Bob paid for — and often he had to pay almost by force because of being a 'guest' — were less than the joy his request gave to the people concerned. Many Greek café owners explained to him that when they first came to small towns they had tentatively introduced a few Greek dishes on their menus, but these were received with distrust, derision or plain ignore.

I do not knock traditional Australian cooking — didn't we invent the lamington? No, we did not invent the pavlova and neither did our New Zealand cousins, though they, like us, cling to this mistaken belief. Although the Americans invented pumpkin pie, we adapted it, and gramma pie its close cousin, to suit our own tastes and added pumpkin scones for good measure. Rosella jam, prickly pear fruit jam, bush currant jelly and tomato jam are virtually indigenous. As to 'muttai' which is green corn boiled (often in corned beef water) and eaten on the cob, the name is certainly local to the New South Wales North Coast.

Les Murray, who contributed 'muttai', also recalls 'pommage', which may be of Scottish origin. It was a coarse porridge of cracked maize, used as a vegetable by needy settlers, and having affinities with the American 'hominy' or 'hominy grits'.

Dishes concocted from corned and/or smoked meat have several names, some regional. 'Red flannel hash' is a dish made from cold minced corned beef. 'Yankee hash' (another dish from Les Murray country) sounds much the same but has melted cheese on top. This dish reminds me that my father, who travelled extensively in America and Europe before World War I, averred that meat dishes named for races or countries should be considered with suspicion because they are *always* made from left-overs; he swore this held true in most corners of the globe. Curiously, this alleged 'rule' does seem to hold.

'Billy Barlow', a popular old bush song* of 1843 hails from Maitland, New South Wales. After many misadventures the unfortunate anti-hero was imprisoned for insolvency:

> Then once more I got free, but in poverty's toil;
> I've no 'cattle for salting', no 'sheep for to boil';
> I can't get a job — though to any I'd stoop,
> If 'twas only the making of 'portable soup'.
> Oh dear, lackaday, oh;
> Pray give some employment to Billy Barlow.

Old Bush Songs, D. Stewart and N. Keesing (eds), Angus & Robertson, 1957.

Here is a recipe for 'portable soup', from *Dainty Dishes for Jewish Families*, May Henry and Kate Halford, Wertheimer, Lea & Co., London, 1902.

> 4 lbs knuckle of veal   3 lbs gravy beef
> 4 lbs shin of beef   3 large onions
>
> Boil the meat in as much water only as will cover it. Remove the marrow from the bones, break them up, add a little spice and the onions, and boil all together. When the meat is done to rags, strain off the liquor and let it stand in a cold place. Take off the fat from the top when cold, and put the soup in a saucepan. Boil it fast and uncovered for 8 hours, stirring it constantly. Pour it into a basin and let it stand a day. Then place the basin in a pan of boiling water on the fire, let it boil again till the soup is thick and ropy. Pour it into flat, plain patty pans to form cakes. When cold turn out on to flannel to dry. Keep the cakes in tin canisters. Use as required, adding boiling water and flavouring.

The Depression of the 1930s caused problems and near or actual starvation was suffered by countless people. But many families would have eaten nicer and more nutritious meals had they known, as many people do now, how to make cheap foods palatable and even the advantages of the sorts of pot herbs that anyone can grow anywhere, including window sills.

I am convinced also that women's magazines were responsible for enlarging the Australian menu, and for improving the appearance of country women and the interiors of Oz homes. A social history of the *Australian Women's Weekly* will prove enlightening.

In the late 1940s, before the gastronomic revolution, I was elected to the committee of a cultural association whose annual dinner was a major affair of great formality in a great university. Soon after my election the menu for this stunning event came under discussion and I, the least and most abashed of newcomers, forever abandoned inappropriate awe as two earnest professors, one headmaster of a famous school, a woman novelist of note and two university lecturers solemnly, and for twenty

117

— repeat twenty — minutes debated the comparative virtues of lemon sago (1/-) or castle pudding (1/6). These, I realised, were mere humans after all considering the relative claims of 'frogs' eyes' versus 'spotted dog', or 'frog-spawn' versus 'flies' cemetery', as some would prefer.

Not so long ago every suburban family had a 'garbo', a 'dunny man' and a 'paper boy' irrespective of the age of the men who delivered papers. 'Bottle-os' had regular rounds and pre-'rotary' housewives recall the clothes-prop man who cried 'clo' prop'. A 'fish-o' was familiar in many areas and, in some, a 'rabbit-o'.* The horse of the Chinese 'vegetable John' pulled a distinctive open cart covered by a brown awning. The 'postie' called twice a day and on Saturday mornings, and the 'milko' poured the daily order into the household billy from his galvanised 'dipper'. In those pre-homogenised times a selfish 'greedy guts' used to 'hog the cream' if no hawk-eyed adult reminded him to 'kindly stir the jug'. Because the milk delivered in this way was 'raw' (not pasteurised) many housewives boiled it, especially in summer or for young children — 'marked milk' was scorched milk.

'What's for lunch/dinner/tea?' 'Stewed roodleums', 'Bread and duck under the table — or duck under the table and bread and pullet.' Some of these expressions that are now domestic jokes originated as brave jests in hard times. 'Hot sun rolls and wind pudding.' 'Wait and see', hence, 'wait and see pudding'. Standby pudding is a quickly-made moulded shape (semolina, milk and eggs) served with jam sauce.

Threatened with such unappetising dishes it is an advantage to be so hungry that: 'I could eat a hollow log full of green ants' (a distinctively northern New South Wales or Queensland expression), or 'I could eat a horse and chase the rider.' 'I could

---

*The South Sydney Rugby League Football Team is known familiarly as the 'Rabbit-os'. South Sydney was the home of the city's rabbit vendors, and they used to release any unsold rabbits on to the football field before their team's Saturday game for spectators to 'bag'.

eat the bum out of an elephant.' 'I could eat a baby's bottom
through a cane chair.'

Even 'bread and scrape' (or scratch), once usually a meagre
film of dripping, but now more often 'marge', is 'yummy' if you're
hungry, and nothing is nicer than when it is your turn for 'a lick
of the dish' — the cake mixture indulgent cooks leave in a basin
for children to spoon out.

Young people who use expressions like the last two, or very
small children, need to learn a few manners. To eat 'keeping
their wings in' or 'their feathers folded' (elbows at sides);* not
'to write on their cabbage' (not to hold their 'eating irons' as

---

*My Great-Aunt Bea commanded small children to sit between
courses with their thumbs hooked over the top edge of the table, hands
underneath. Try it yourself — you have to sit straight and without fid-
getting.

one would hold a pencil); not to make slurping sounds 'like a cow with its foot in a bog'.

In many families children's opinions of food are neither sought nor welcome at the meal table though their elders and betters are allowed to say that the nice hot soup 'just warms the cockles of my heart', or that a welcome 'cuppa' (tea) when one is 'fanging for a drink' 'just wets my sides'. This is the direct opposite of the first beer that goes so quickly down a male throat it fails 'to wet me sides'. Soup 'like dishwater' is better disregarded. Kids who 'do (or chuck) an Oliver' and ask for more when more is not available may be advised 'little fish are sweet'.

Mount Morgan, Queensland, gave gold, copper and, indirectly, cheap Persian petrol to the world. Also 'gooligum' and 'the cutter'. 'Gooligum' is golden syrup and butter mixed by each diner on the side of a plate with a bread and butter knife to the desired brown stickiness. It is then applied to puftaloons, or puftaloonies (fried scones) and only puftaloons — not to toast or ordinary scones. 'The cutter' was a billy of beer, and the practise of 'running the cutter' allowed miners coming off shift to drink, sitting on logs laid on the grass, on their way home. The cutter was passed from man to man. Boys were given 7d to fetch a cutter from a hotel (6d for the beer, 1d tip). Some wives sent a child for a cutter which the husband drank at home with his evening meal. Some men rubbed cheese on the inside of the base of the cutter — this was said to reduce the amount of froth in the can. 'Running the cutter' ceased with the introduction and enforcement of stricter licensing laws at the time of World War I.

The Queensland coal mining town of Blair Athol gave the world 'eleveners' — the morning break, or recess in a school day or 'playlunch' as it might be called further south. But in Queensland 'eleveners' have disappeared in favour of the universal 'little lunch' to eat during the morning; 'big lunch' is eaten at lunch time. An unnerved southern visitor to a Queensland school experiences considerable culture shock when, at about 10.30, a bell rings and a mature, dignified teacher invites her to the staff room for 'little lunch'.

Virtually continent-wide dad, if he does mining work, still takes his crib unless he prefers the delights of 'takeaways' that are often as 'salty as Lot's Wife'.

During the 1914-18 War, when patriotism in Australia knew few bounds of either commonsense or logic, anything 'Hunnish' was eschewed and, together with countless names of people and places, the humble German sausage (sometimes known as Fritz), a staple for sandwiches then as now, had to be amended. First it was called 'Belgian' sausage, then in many places, 'Devon' sausage. In central Queensland it is 'Windsor' sausage, although whether this is a compliment to a long vanished manufacturer, or to the British Royal Family, is unclear. In Western Australia it is 'Poloni'.

And speaking of the sandwich. In New South Wales a sandwich is two slices of bread with a filling between; these slices can be cut in halves to produce either two rectangles or two triangles, and again in quarters to yield four of either in a dainty size. Pity the uninitiated New South Welshperson in Victoria (and other areas) who thinks how *cheap* sandwiches are in that state. Not so. The cost of a sandwich in such benighted backwoods pays for one slice of bread only. Pity even more the unfortunate US or Japanese tourist who orders a sandwich and receives some variant of the above, instead of his anticipated elaborate meal on bread known as a 'Dagwood' or 'Bumstead Special' to Australians. 'Open-face' or 'Danish' sandwiches still do not approach the genuine American article (and still less the Scandinavian one). Australian sandwiches, if made of thick bread, are 'doorsteps' or 'slabs'.

It is necessary nowadays to understand that a 'bun' may in some places be, well, a bun; a bun with a shiny glazed top and a bit of spice and dried fruit in its composition. But the name may also be a shortened form of 'hamburger bun', which is a plain bread roll of flattened shape made to contain a hamburger, cheeseburger, chickenburger or fishburger. As for shops selling both hamburgers *and* steakburgers, I have never been game to investigate since my understanding is that a hamburger is made of minced beef. A hamburger made of minced ham, so far as I know, lacks both inventor and title.

121

Only South Australia, I think, has 'Jubilee Loaf', a yeast loaf choc-a-bloc with dried fruit and citrus peel.

One colloquialism seems to have vanished along with a size and shape of loaf that used to be standard in Australian shops. It was baked in a two-pound tin and allowed to rise fully. If you can find one now it will be called a 'country loaf'. Its slices looked like this: ⬭ ⬭←CHURCH ⬭ ← CHAPEL In pre 'pop up' days when mum made breakfast toast under the griller of a Nu-Kooka gas stove, four slices of this bread fitted nicely in each batch. Half of each fragrant slice was the equivalent of a piece of pre-sliced, hygienically wrapped cardboard that now passes for bread. Some people liked the top half whose crust was very brown even before toasting; some preferred the lower portion. So, 'church or chapel?' was *the* breakfast-time question.

Bubba in the high chair splashes around 'making a pudding of her porridge', which is more likely to be something puréed from a tin. Bubba being contrary, however, she is just as likely to spread it all over the place, or spit it out, even if mum has taken the trouble to mash and strain something home-cooked.

'Come on,' helpful dad coaxes. 'This'll make your hair curl.' In goes a spoonful. 'This'll put skin on your back like velvet; and now, one more spoonful for Uncle Frank, and just *one* more down your little red lane.' Bubba, sceptical, if not downright

infuriated, musters all those spoonsful from fat cheeks and lets dad have them right between the eyes.

Family mealtimes are no win situations. 'You've all got bionic mouths,' sighs a harassed young mother. Either everyone is 'hoeing in' without appreciation of 'enough is as good as a feast' ('You think more of your gut than your God' was a reproach in more strictly Protestant days,), or else they are inventing horrible names for what they eat:

Adam and Eve on a raft are two fried eggs on toast, and wreck 'em (break the yolks)
hen fruit/cackleberries are eggs
stodge/sudden death are cakes
snail [cake] is swiss roll
social gravel is coffee crystals
Bundaberg mud is refined sugar of poor colour (a World War II term that has persisted)
bill poster's paste is custard
BDs are baked dinners
marked milk is scorched milk
penny lines are penny lollies
snags/bangers/mystery bags are sausages

If family food terms seem overseasoned they are bland by comparison with boarding school inventions. These are so various, ephemeral and localised and, frankly, so undomestic, that I despair of being fair to boarding schools across the continent and have decided against more than a token 'Dead man's leg', a sort of meat-loaf; 'Hitler's toe', fried-up Devon sausage; 'Yarra mud and dandruff', chocolate blancmange with desiccated coconut.

After the meal is over food that disagrees ('I like it but it doesn't like me'), is an obvious cause of colliwobbles, grumbly tumbly, and dog's disease, which can also be influenza and other ailments. Tainted food may lead to 'the gullivers' (*Gulliver's travels* — diarrhoea), or the 'trots' or to an unfortunate

123

sufferer 'bringing it up from his boots'. In other words it makes you feel 'as crook as Rookwood'.*

I LIKE AEROPLANE JELLY!
AEROPLANE JELLY FOR ME!
I LIKE IT FOR DINNER, I LIKE IT FOR TEA ...

Next to 'Waltzing Matilda' this is Australia's best known song — both celebrate tucker!

---

*Rookwood is a large Sydney cemetery.

11

While I live I'll crow

A SCREW LOOSE WITHOUT ENOUGH SENSE TO
COME IN OUT OF THE RAIN

Writing all over the page like a
drunken spider

Wouldn't it rot your socks

Muscle bound behind the ears

A BLIND MAN ON A GALLOPING HORSE
WOULD BE GLAD TO SEE IT

The language of Familyspeak, I hope, is entirely unreliable as an indicator of widespread national traits and personal qualities. I cannot believe that Australians are a nation of liars, bludgers and lunatics or that they are overwhelmingly greedy, lazy and impertinent. Rather, they seem to be all of those things to exasperated loved ones from time to time and especially when very young, constantly under adult feet and trying to learn everything from how to tie a shoelace, use a knife and fork, sew a seam, weed the garden, mop a floor, write a school composition, boil an egg or hammer in a nail.

The girl who mislays her mother's carefully prepared shopping list and does her best from imperfect memory only seems to lack 'enough brains to make her head ache' nor is she actually 'a screw loose' or without 'enough sense to come in out of the rain'. More to the point is her brother's remark that she'd 'forget her head if it wasn't screwed on'. Her aunt sums up: 'You wouldn't know if it was Thursday or Anthony Horderns.'

Like the ubiquitous Bondi tram, Anthony Horderns, a Sydney emporium, was renowned nearly Australia-wide. And like the tram, although Anthony Horderns is now defunct, it is immortalised in colloquial speech. Anthony Horderns was an immense Sydney department store covering an entire city block of over an acre on the site of the early brickfields that supplied walls for buildings and a name to 'the brickfielder', a blustery southerly wind that once blew grit and dust far and wide over infant Sydney. Country visitors considered a visit to 'Horderns' an indispensable ritual during 'a trip to town', and city people shopped there for every imaginable commodity under one roof. It was Horderns' mail order catalogue, however, the nearest thing to Sears Roebuck this country ever had, that ensured its most far reaching fame; from its pages country people ordered everything 'from a needle to an anchor' according to the store's proud, and proudly truthful, motto. The firm's trademark was a spreading fig tree over the slogan: 'While I live I'll grow'. The Hordern family had traded in Sydney since the 1830s, and it has been suggested that the famous slogan derived from the popular convict versifier, Frank the Poet, who boasted defiantly, 'While I live I'll crow.'

There was a spooky angle to the firm's demise, although its decline was caused by altering shopping habits, the deterioration of the area of inner Sydney where the building was located, and other non-occult reasons. A huge old fig tree stood alone in a paddock at the summit of the notorious Razorback Mountain road near Picton and was a welcome landmark to early coachmen, teamsters and pioneer motorists whose engines inevitably and often boiled during this long climb on the only direct inland route between Sydney, the southern highlands and, eventually, Victoria. This famous old tree was popularly called the 'Anthony Horderns Tree' by generations of travellers until it was struck by lightning and lingered, half-killed, a pitiful jumble of sagging branches. Despite the best efforts of tree surgeons it died a few years later. This melancholy decline virtually coincided with the death throes of the far-famed store.

'Everything from a needle to an anchor' or 'Anthony Horderns to an anchor' still signifies *absolutely everything* in colloquial speech. Once, I walked through the cavernous carpet department, past a display of fruit-bottling equipment, from end to end of the Fine Arts Department (and Fine Arts were pre-

128

cisely that — treasures of antique furniture, glass and china; pictures and sculpture new and recent) *en route* for kitchenware. Somewhere between Georgian silver tureens and everyday saucepans an area was cordoned off for a Persian cat show, and Persian kittens were on offer. It was in an Anthony Horderns lift, an intricate cage of wrought iron grille-work driven by a uniformed man, that my fascinated father heard and saw the following:

'Where's 'ats?' asked the customer.
'First floor madam,' said the lift-driver, bringing the cage to a thumping halt, 'and turn right.' And turn right she did, on the floor of the lift.

Obviously she 'had rocks in her head', thus resembling bored, 'thick' or 'wool gathering' school students who sit in front of their teachers 'like lumps of suet', and often produce careless handwriting 'all over the page like a drunken spider'. In the playground the clumsy child 'born with two left thumbs' or 'all thumbs' will very likely be a 'butter fingers', too. The youngster who trips over his own shoes 'has two left feet'. Whether or not life was meant to be easy* it is certainly often unfair and the clever child, 'a real head' who 'knows his onions' frequently gets slapped down with withering sarcasm: 'Ask Sheila, she knows everything!'

It is suggested to dopes that they are not worth their salt or 'the paper you're printed on' so 'pull your socks up, PDQ' (pretty damn quick), or 'POQ' (piss off quick).

The opposite of a dull or lethargic person can be equally foolish by wasting energy in over-exertion or by performing tasks in ill-prepared and unproductive ways: these are the people who go at a job 'like a bull at a gate' or 'go in and out like a fiddler's elbow' or over-react like 'a one-armed fiddler with the itch'. People who rush around aimlessly resemble 'a headless (or

---

*'Life wasn't meant to be easy.' A widely used vogue phrase, used by an Australian Prime Minister, Malcolm Fraser. His wife, Tamara, is fond of saying, 'Wouldn't it rot your socks.'

Liberté, egalité, chicken dinner

decapitated) chook'. This image was particularly vivid to generations of Australians whether they lived in city suburbs or 'out in the sticks'. I include the phrase, although it has been widely collected already, because several people wrote to stress the appeal it made to their imagination as children when the beheading of poultry for the table was a familiar event that horrified and, at the same time, fascinated them.

Until recently, countless suburban families kept a few chooks up the yard (in a 'chook house', naturally); they enjoyed fresh eggs and killed an occasional old boiler or redundant cockerel for the pot. My father did not decapitate his chooks but slit their throats over a hole dug in the earth and then hung them by the legs, for a while, to bleed thoroughly. Most people, however, used a tomahawk to chop the heads off birds on a block also used for chopping wood, or chips for the bath-heater, and then released the victim to flap around in circles while its severed head uttered feeble squeaks until, after a few seconds, both were still. Sensitive youngsters found the procedure distressing — even if you didn't watch you heard the flurry and squawking of the capture and often the dying bird had been a well-loved pet during its earlier career.

One of my childhood neighbours, a widow, was unable to face the horrid task until her son-in-law invented a machine that was for all the world like a French revolutionary guillotine in miniature. Now all she had to do was catch her victim, stretch its neck across a steel block, fasten a wire loop that held it in place, grab the string that raised the blade, turn her back, release the string and, after a reasonable interval, pick up her Sunday dinner.

Digression: these post mortem antics of chooks had an affinity with a popular puzzle sentence: 'King Charles walked and talked half an hour after his head was cut off.' (Punctuate it.) Puzzles were popular: 'What's the difference between a duck?' 'One of its legs is both the same.'; 'How many beans make five?'; 'How long is a piece of string?'; 'How many wells make a river?' (The answer to this one was, as a rule, three — 'Well, well, well.') Then there was 'Which weighs most — a ton of coal or a ton of feathers?'; and, to be translated, '*Pas d'elle y Rhône que nous*?' (Paddle your own canoe), and '*Caesar adsum iam forte*' (Caesar had some jam for tea).

Nowadays, few suburban councils permit householders to keep hens for reasons of noise control and hygiene. No longer do people who have to be up by sunrise judge approaching dawn by first one, and then another, crowing rooster. Electronic bleeps or radio sound are less euphonious substitutes and can be truly alarming. On the morning of 1981 when news broke of the attempted assassination of President Reagan, a politically unconservative Sydney woman was awoken by her clock radio several seconds after the headline news had been given. 'General Haig has assumed full control of the government,' she heard, and nearly 'flew off her perch'. Somewhere near inner Sydney a defiant rooster still crows and, from time to time, considerably exercises the letter columns of the *Sydney Morning Herald* when Balmain citizens complain that its matutinal arias seriously disturb their rest — 'noise pollution' is the 'in' word. Argument rages about whether the anachronistic cock inhabits Goat Island or lives illegally in a Balmain backyard. If indeed this rooster lives on Goat Island either he has possibly the

131

'solid concrete north of the necktie'

loudest crow ever recorded or Balmain folk are notably light sleepers; the island is a considerable distance from their huddled houses across a stretch of harbour water.

To revert to endlessly fascinating topics: stupidity and laziness, which is stupidity's kissing cousin. The exasperating person who is 'mad as a meat ant (or meat axe)', 'silly as a tin of worms (or a cut snake)' is 'muscle-bound behind the ears' or made of 'solid concrete north of the necktie' makes more sensible people suppose that 'if your brains were barbed wire you couldn't fence a shit house' or 'if they were gunpowder they'd never part your hair and blow your hat off'. Someone who does something mildly silly or eccentric is 'nutty as a fruit cake' but she who demonstrates absolute or outrageous pottiness is 'Rats in the attic! Bang! Bang!'

Everyone knows that the longer you put an unwelcome task 'on the long finger', the longer it will take.* Of the most obsti-

---

*It has been suggested that this term derives from lace-making.

nately lazy people it has to be said 'they're not worth their weight in rocking horse dirt' and that they come perilously close to 'wanting pin-holes in their coffin', which is the ultimate denigratory term for the sort of bludger who manages to 'lie doggo' while others 'do the heavy'.

When sarcasm, invective, invention and all else fails mum, like her mother before her, falls back on, 'Just you wait till your father gets home and hears about this! Then there'll be "wigs on the green"/"fur and feathers flying"/"a taste of strop" (even now, when disposable razors are universal).'

Scornful expressions for bludgers are the other side of the coinages reserved for real triers and/or genuine 'pipsqueaks' (small children) who are inexpertly learning to master skills. A range of kindly encouragement recognises that, after all, 'where there's a will there's a way', and the important thing is that 'if at first you don't succeed, try, try, try again', a quotation that perpetuates the refrain of a long-forgotten nineteenth century moral rhyme.

Try Again

'Tis a lesson you should heed,
Try again;
If at first you don't succeed,
Try again;
Then your courage should appear,
For if you will persevere,
You will conquer, never fear,
Try again.

Once or twice, though you should fail
Try again;
If you would at last prevail,
Try again;
If we strive, 'tis no disgrace
Though we do not win the race;
What should we do in that case?
Try again.

If you find your task is hard,
Try again;
Time will bring you your reward,
Try again;
All that other folk can do,
Why, with patience, may not you?
Only keep this rule in view,
Try again.

E. Hickson

'A blind man on a galloping horse would never see it (or would be glad to see it)' reassures a beginner that some small fault is barely noticeable and won't affect the quality of the finished artefact; according to many correspondents this phrase is usually reserved for girls learning to knit or sew.

12

I am a traveller bound for foreign countries*

*Duty free identification, Honolulu International Airport.

TAKE A LONG WALK OFF A SHORT PIER

Full as a goog

'Let's toddle along for a spot;
I'm thirsty.'

The streets are full of sailors and not a
whore in the house has been washed

ROLLS-CANARDLY

*Carniver drink or a bad attack of the
gimmies*

SNOT FAIR

Over centuries the English language travelled to, and reflected the diversity of, that vanished empire on which the sun never set. Travelling words acquire variegated histories. In Australia a colourful example is 'knock'. Australians are ironically proud of one of its locally acquired meanings and of our reputation as a land of 'knockers' in which sense the word is a portmanteau term embracing elements of scepticism, rejection, complaint, jeering, carping, unreasonable criticism and a few more.

One meaning of 'knock' recorded by the *Oxford English Dictionary* from England in 1598 is 'to copulate'. In this sense, but with later variations, it acclimatised in Australia and also in America and caused some devastating misunderstandings among the descendants of its original users in each country.

When a young Australian man 'puts the hard word on' a girl who does not welcome his sexual importunities she will 'knock him back' (tell him to 'go and jump in the lake' or 'take a long walk off a short pier' — or worse). But if she agrees to his pleadings he may later boast to his mates that he 'knocked her off'.

Girls who do agree run the risk of pregnancy; such a girl in America may find herself 'knocked up'. But when an Australian announces she is 'knocked up' she means tired out, usually after a strenuous day's work or energetic sport. During the 'Yank invasion' of Australia during World War II these trans-Pacific variations were awkward and even sad. 'Hank asked me to go to the Troc [The Trocadero, a Sydney dance hall] tonight but I said I just couldn't — it was a helluva day at work and I felt real knocked up.' For years afterwards she wondered why Hank, who seemed such a nice boy and 'real gone' on her, 'dropped her like a hot cake' and 'shot through' so precipitately that she 'never saw his heels for dust'. As for Hank, who was half in love with her, and may have become devotedly so, he spent a miserable few weeks, and anxious, too, remembering an impetuous half hour under a Moreton Bay fig tree in the Dom. [The Sydney Domain, an unfenced and dimly lit parkland.]

In and out of wartime many an impetuous occasion results in a baby born out of wedlock. In New South Wales unmarried mothers or deserted wives could claim various allowances and benefits from 'the Welfare' (Child Welfare Department) provided they followed necessary statutory procedures, one of which was to 'slap a writ' on the putative father. If he could be found, usually by the police, a magistrate assessed the amount of 'maintenance' he 'was up for'. If he fell behind with his payments he was liable to a term in prison. The word 'maintenance' was widely mispronounced 'main-*tain*-ance'. Some city jails were overcrowded with men 'in for main*tain*ance'. It was a silly and self-perpetuating system because these incarcerated 'knockers-off' were precluded from earning wages at their ordinary jobs and fell even further behind with their obligatory dues. These procedures have been altered and reformed long since.

Child endowment payments are made routinely in respect of all eligible Australian children, irrespective of family income or legitimacy. The endowment is also widely mispronounced as one word 'thendowment'. 'Thendowment' cheques are paid directly to mothers and for some less fortunate women are their only certain cash income, being independent of the whims, meanness or intemperate habits of unsatisfactory fathers.

Australian general slang has countless terms for drunkenness most of which are known to women and used by them; but a few of these terms seem to be used more often by, or about women than by or about men, and other possible differences of usage emerged from my correspondence and radio talk back programmes. 'Full as a family jerry (or po)' seems to be particularly favoured by women and to have had a long currency; people recall their mothers and grandmothers using the expression and it is also in current use although chamber pots, or pos are no longer necessary items in most bedrooms, and hence no longer favourite objects of vulgar humour.

Did an anonymous contributor to the *Bathurst Sentinel* in 1879 intend vulgar humour or high drama with a poem called 'A Mother's Love', which is surely the most curious verse in Australian poesy? I cannot resist quoting it here.*

> A child sat aloft on the windy tree
> And crieth, "O, mother, I want to p.,"
> "Fain would I p." cried the child in wo,
> "O fetch for me, mother, the rounded po."
>
> The mother paused not, but straightway sped,
> With a breaking heart, to her lonely bed,
> And fell on her knees and fumbled there
> For that much-used vessel of earthenware.
>
> But horror! Why starts she and trembles so?
> It cannot be at the sight of the po,
> For it is not there, but in its stead,
> Her liege lord's bleeding and trunkless head.
>
> Quick she recovers from shock and fright,
> But she looks not again on the bloody sight.
> Her thoughts are still with the child in the tree,
> Who crieth, "O, mother, I fain would p."

---

*Comic Australian Verse, chosen by Geoffrey Lehmann, Angus & Robertson, 1972.

The Family po

> And she rushes forth with her soul aflame
> To her next-door neighbour, a high-born dame,
> She telleth her story, and both in wo
> Bear forth to the child the rounded po.

'Full as a goog' must be nearly as venerable and long-lived as 'full as a family po'. Standard compilations of colloquial speech give 'full as a goog' as a term for drunkenness, and it is used in this way among men. In the 1950s a disreputable-looking old 'wino' used to weave along the Sydney footpath near my office muttering to himself. One day, being inquisitive, I paced beside him, listening. Over and over he mumbled, 'I'm full as a goog, I'm full as a goog, I'm full as a goog ...' Several women, however, gave 'full as a goog' as a term meaning replete with food and many insisted that while 'full as a boot' (also widespread) invariably denoted insobriety, 'full as a goog' — a 'goog' being a 'googy egg'* in nursery speech — always and only applied to food. As my mother would have said, 'You pays your money and you takes your choice.'

'A spot', meaning an alcoholic drink, seems by the 1980s to be a predominantly feminine usage. A man may ask a woman whether she'd like 'a spot' but I doubt men use the term among themselves nowadays; in the 1930s it was a vogue phrase used by both sexes and perhaps owing a good deal to P. G. Wodehouse — it seems to go with plus fours and an exaggerated 'English' accent along the lines of 'I say old bean, let's toddle along for a spot, eh? Jolly thirsty weather, don't y' know!' One woman wrote that in the 1930s, in Sydney, 'a spot' was always a small

---

*See also p. 167.

glass of sherry; however, since the 1940s it has referred to drinks of all kinds as, too, does 'a short snort'. S/he who suffers from '4 X Fever' (Fourex is a Queensland beer) has not necessarily become intoxicated from beer alone.

I have not heard of any expression specific to a drunken female apart from 'tiddley'. In older generations women who imbibed to excess were often spoken about rather protectively by other women: Mary is 'flushed' again or 'a bit astray this evening', or 'a little upset' or 'rather excited'. One consequence

a few spots later...

of equality between the sexes seems to be the gradual disappearance of this sort of convention — today if Mary drinks too much she is 'smashed' or 'stinko' or whatever the 'in' phrase is.

Solitary or 'closet' drinking is, according to sociological research, a hazard of life in suburban 'boxes' whose red brick and tile are said to hide alarming numbers of lonely and neurotic housewives 'hooked' on valium and other anti-depressant pills, or the bottle. Better adjusted or less lonely women put a braver face on moments of frustration, despair or just plain muddle. One letter explained, 'An old family friend uses the expression "won't be long, won't be Lewisham" when life gets frantic, the implication being that she's headed for the asylum, not the ordinary hospital.' (Lewisham Hospital, in an inner Sydney suburb of that name, is a general hospital; mental patients are nursed elsewhere.)

Phrases and words alter their meanings between countries, within countries and across time and also as a consequence of neighbourhood or family traditions. Everyone, throughout life, and often unconsciously, must accommodate to the speech customs of friends, associates and marriage partners. Certain changes seem to result from forms of censorship. I earlier mentioned the schoolteacher who substituted 'spit' for 'wee' in a phrase used by his grandmother and later by him to his pupils.

Why certain colloquialisms 'catch on' and become popular, long-lived and widespread, while others that sound equally amusing or apt have a restricted currency or are 'here today and gone tomorrow' is mysterious. One man wrote,

My mother used to use a saying which I have never heard from anyone else. It obviously originated from the convict era and she, no doubt, learned it from her own mother whose early years would almost have reached back to that period. When she wanted to point out how one's fortunes could change overnight for the worse she used to illustrate this with the saying 'Here today and tomorrow picking oakum' ... the picking of oakum for the caulking of ships' decks was one of the occupations of the convicts of our early period ... I would be interested to know whether you have ever come across it before.

I have not come across it before, and the picking of oakum as a prison occupation was not confined to early Australian convicts — what interests me, though, is that such a graphic expression is so little known and used.

One Sydney family of Cornish/Scottish extraction has several salty phrases that unaccountably seem to have been unique to it for several generations. 'Not every day we kill a pig and give the gut to the poor of the parish,' they exclaim with satisfaction after 'throwing' a good party, and instead of 'hurry up' they say 'The streets are full of sailors and not a whore in the house washed!' A variant of this phrase was used in the 1950s by two lesbian women who said it was in current use among Sydney prostitutes of that time: 'Not a kid in the house [brothel] dressed for school [ready for work], not a piss-pot emptied and the streets are full of sailors.' An elderly woman who has not enjoyed a function exclaims 'It's no show without Punch'. A young woman laughs about a friend who was so furious when she noticed her husband flirting with a girl at a party that 'she nearly flew off the handle'.

When I began collecting colloquial speech for this book people reported examples that sounded as if they were in such restricted use that I doubted whether I should include them. An example is the 'canardlies'. I was told of an uncle who used this word in two ways: if a newly-engaged girl flaunted her engagement ring in an exaggerated fashion, or if people drew his attention to their new possessions very blatantly, he would exclaim, sarcastically 'Hold off! I canardly [see it.]' Or, more puzzling, he also spoke of a 'rollscanardly' which was said to go down one hill easily but could hardly get up the next. I, as it turned out quite wrongly and being 'a bit thick in the clear',

143

supposed a 'rollscanardly' to be a fat person. Not so, for the word appeared in a later letter spelled 'Rolls-canardly' and was explained as a car which can easily roll down one hill but hardly grind up the next. Not only was the puzzle solved, but it began to seem as if the 'canardlies' may be quite well known.

Closely related to the 'canardly' is the 'canniver'. The 'canniver' is a child suffering from what some families might call 'a bad attack of the gimmies'. Such children are frequently accused of being natives of the western Victorian town of Kaniva. Another place from which small children may come, or that they frequently visit, is 'Snot Fair'. A tearful, little boy at McLaren Vale in South Australia who, circa 1940 was heard protesting, 'I tore a sluddy great hole in my pants, that I never', sounds like a denizen of 'Snot Fair'.

13

Half English—half something else

SHICKERED IN A SHEMOZZLE

Ha-ha pigeon

Vegetabili and the milchibar

The Hebi

DON'T MAKE FAXEN

Since white settlement, Australian general slang has contained words and phrases from languages other than English. Some of these words were acquired from, or shared with, English and American colloquial speech. For instance 'shiker'* or 'shickered' for drunk is a direct borrowing from the Yiddish *shikker*, as is 'mozzle' for luck which comes from the Yiddish *mazel* (pronounced to rhyme with nozzle). Thus, an Australian usage noted by Baker, 'Kronk mozzle' for bad luck, comes from the Yiddish *krenk*, an illness, or *kronk*, to have an illness (Baker's spelling).

One woman who wrote to me grew up in Kings Cross during the 1930s and has remembered three colourful phrases used by one of the neighbours, a Jewish woman. In my correspondent's spelling and interpretation these were: a *schmozzle* (a mess); a real *Shemile* or *Chemile* (a very naive person); a *missamushia* (my correspondent was not sure of the meaning).

These are my explanations of the three examples.
Shemozzl or *shlemozzl* (pronounced sheh-mozzle or shleh-

*Yiddish spellings and definitions in this section are from *The Joys of Yiddish*, Leo Rosten, Penguin, 1971.

147

mozzle — rhyming with den-nozzle): Leo Rosten, who is an American expert on the Yiddish language, says, 'these words are not Yiddish, and not Yinglish, but slang used by our cousins in England and Ireland ... they are often spelled and pronounced like the Yiddish *shlimazl* to which they bear not the slightest resemblance.'

A *shemozzle* is an uproar, a fight, and can also mean to decamp or abscond. (It is notably used by race-course touts says Rosten.) A *shlimazl*, however, is a born loser. According to Rosten 'when a shlimazl winds a clock, it stops; when he kills a chicken, it walks; when he sells umbrellas, the sun comes out; when he manufactures shrouds, people stop dying.'

Shlemiel (pronounced *shle*-meal — to rhyme with reveal): indeed a naive person. A simpleton might be said to 'have the brains of a schlemiel — when he falls on his back he breaks his nose.'

Missamushia: such a gorgeous word that one is not surprised it has lived in a memory for some fifty years. Its meaning is a bit less certain than the other two words, but I imagine the woman who used it had in mind one or other of the following three Yiddish phrases.

Mishegoss literally means insanity but is more often used to describe tomfoolery, absurd belief, nonsense. It derives from *meshuga* which is the Hebrew word meaning insane; meshuga, too, is more widely used in Yiddish to mean wildly and extravagantly bonkers — 'rats in the attic bang! bang!' as Australian speakers might say. A crazy man is a *meshuggener*. A crazy woman is a *meshuggeneh.*

It is just possible, however, that the word remembered as *Missamushia* was 'mish-mash' (as the *Oxford English Dictionary* spells it), or *mish-mosh* as Yiddish usage and custom prefers. A *mish-mosh* is a state of utter confusion.

Another widely used Yiddish expression — also present-day German — is *gesundheit* (pronounced ge-zund-hite). This means, literally, 'health' and is said, in the same way that English-speakers say 'bless you', to someone who sneezes.

There is a fair degree of *mish-mosh* in a lot of speech used in Australia. Aborigines, for instance, have incorporated some non-Aboriginal words into the *patois* they speak, and these ways of speech reflect wide regional differences in languages and dialects across the country. They have incorporated Aboriginal words in the forms of English they use, also. In the 1950s a Thursday Island grandmother of Sri Lankan/Anglo-Saxon descent, who was born at about the turn of the century, had some unusual expressions. To someone 'flapping around' or over-reacting: 'Stop ginning around!' 'You're like a gin in bloomers!'; 'You're carrying on like a gin at a christening!' To someone offering the excuse, 'but I thought ...' — who had been thoughtless: 'You know what thought did — he thought he'd shat himself but he hadn't.' People or things that would not mix were 'like shit to an oily rag'.

Germans, Greeks, Italians and, no doubt, other migrant groups have altered their speech very much as the Aborigines have done. Because German and Italian speaking people have been established in some parts of Australia over many generations, their usages tend to have been studied more closely. But even recent migrants acquire colloquial forms; for instance some Greek and Italian migrants who have come from areas where fenced, individual yards and gardens are unknown, speak of *to backyardou* (Greek) and *la fensa* (Italian). Italians working on the Snowy River scheme called the kookaburra, or 'laughing jackass', 'Ha-ha Pigeon'.

Anne Lloyd, a linguist working in Rockhampton, has provided most of the German and Italian examples that follow. Over several generations, some German speakers have incorporated such words as 'beach', 'surf', 'gum-tree', 'drover', 'council', 'township' and 'tractor'. Often, gender is assigned to this kind of usage: *die fire, der creek, die road.* Assigned gender is an indication of integration in the adopting language. Verbs are transferred also: *trainen, relieven, joinen, driven, cutten.* Instead of the normal German tag question '*Nicht wahr?*' Australian German has invented '*Ist es?*' ('Is it?') and '*Tut er?*' ('Does he?'). Australian German has also 'invented' some phrases that are literal translations from English and serve to fill gaps where no equivalent

Backyardou

German phrase exists: 'For better or for worse' becomes *Für schlecter oder besser.*

Australian Italian uses some words that have a different meaning in Italian:

Australian Italian		Italian	
lodare	to load (in preference to Italian *caricare*)	*lodare*	to praise
fattoria	factory	*fattoria*	farm
parenti	parents	*parenti*	relatives in general
relativi	relatives (coined because of the restricted meaning of *parenti*)		

Australian Italian also contains some words that have no literal meaning in Italian.

Australian Italian		Italian	
arvesto	harvest	*raccolto*	harvest
landa	land	*terra*	land
nido	I need	*ho bisogno*	I need

The first two Australian Italian words have no meaning in Italian, but *nido* in the original language means 'birds' nest'. *Vegetabili* has been invented instead of *verdura* for vegetables, and *russiano* instead of *russo* for Russian. The kind of words that have been coined for uniquely Australian concepts include *billicàno* (billycan); *tièbi* (TAB); and *milchibar* (milkbar).

I borrowed the title of this chapter from the poet Les Murray. Les and his wife, Valerie, contributed phrases that their family uses and which derive from Valerie's background both as a teacher of English as a second language and because of her mixed-language family background: her mother was Swiss, her father Hungarian. With Les Murray's permission I substantially quote his words:

Schmückedein: in the Murray household 'kitschy' objects are *Schmückedein*, deriving from *Schmücke dein Heim* (Decorate your Home), which is the common sign over shooting galleries and similar sideshows at fairgrounds in Switzerland.

trouser: in the singular, i.e. 'he was wearing a trouser' not a pair of trousers, or 'wearing trousers'.

es laat: Swiss German, literally 'it gives way'. Used humorously when demonstrating that something you meant to discard anyway really has had it. Ripping a worn-out but beloved shirt straight up the back, a cheerfully merciless wife will say *'Sehsch, es laat!'* ('See, it tears; no more wear in that!')

bicyclist: a high and mighty crawler, a toady. 'One who bows to that which is above while treading on that which is below'. From the Hungarian *biciklista* (pronounced bitz-ik-lish-to), this is old Budapest slang.

Once: translation of the ubiquitous German adverb *mal, einmal.* For example, 'I'll have to go up to Newcastle once and see him.' Also heard in the Barossa Valley, South Australia.

To dress: to dress a bed is to make a bed; *to open* a bed means to pull back the covers.

Schön: something more intimate, warmer, and even more beautiful than beautiful, which is its exact English translation; the youngest child of a loving family might be not only beautiful, but also *schön.*

Gigampfe: a Swiss verb, pronounced *gi-gampfa.* It is a splendid example of a useful word existing in one language and having no exact equivalent in another. One example might be the French *en rapport* which means so much more than 'to be in sympathy with'. *Gigampfe* is 'to lean back on a chair and rock on the rear legs to the great detriment of the chair and peril to the rocking party'. It can also mean 'to see-saw'.

Ohrfeige: as in 'simple as an *Ohrfeige*', 'simple as a box on the ears'. This is an ordinary German idiom, and the word is pronounced *or*-faiga.

Faxen: faces, in the sense of grimaces: 'Don't make faxen!'

Szegen: pronounced *sag-ehn* to rhyme with nag-pain. This is the Hungarian word for 'poor' in the sense of something or some-

one worthy of pity. In the Australian household of the Murray family it is used of things which have sagged or lost their crispness. For example: 'Poor candle. It's melted. *Szegen* candle.'
Prost, prosit: 'Your health'. This German toast is used a good deal in the family. Similarly, many Jewish people use the toast, *'L'haim'* ('To life'), and Scandinavians in Australia perpetuate *skol*.

Les Murray goes on to say that lots of other non-English words, usually from standard German, make ephemeral guest-appearances in the speech of his family. Foreign usages do not carry over to or affect his writing because they belong to a completely different sphere of life.

14

Back to Bunyah

ITS MOMENTS LIKE THESE

Two chances — Buckley's and none

The plastic doohickey

'Geez, Les, you put on lots of condition'

PICKING FLY DIRT FROM PEPPER

Neither me arse nor me elbow

A CRACKER COW

Y ou could ride to Bourke and back on that knife and it wouldn't cut your bottom' is an instance of colloquial speech that is tied loosely to a locality. Unless the hearer knows that Bourke is a far distant place the phrase is meaningless. 'Crook as Rookwood' can only mean 'very crook indeed' if the hearer shares the speaker's knowledge that Rookwood is a large cemetery near Sydney. If I say a person is too stupid to know 'whether it is Thursday or Anthony Horderns', or that, being astray as to wits she has 'gone to Gowings' my words only have meaning if my auditor understands that these are famous Sydney shops. Furthermore, 'gone to Gowings' may not have much impact on people too young to remember a long-continued advertising campaign of which 'gone to Gowings' was the slogan. On the other hand, 'it's moments like these' or 'don't forget!' would be understood now because Minties ('it's moments like these you need Minties') or Aeroguard (insect repellent — 'don't forget the Aeroguard') are promoted continent wide. Unaccountably, however, a few localised phrases seem as immortal as the Bondi tram. The widespread general slang phrase 'Buckley's' or 'Buckley's chance' very likely originated with the Melbourne department store Buckley & Nunn: 'You've got two chances, Buckley's and none.'

While I compiled this book I realised that unless I could somehow publicise my quest to every corner of the continent, and even every one of its inhabited off-shore islands, inevitably I would miss excellent local or regional examples. When eventually I was able to research for two months in central Queensland, and by radio in South Australia and, thanks to Elizabeth Jolley's students, in Western Australia, I was struck by the homogeneity of domestic colloquial speech. Some usages are peculiar to localities and regions — they are noted throughout this book. But many words and phrases are much more widespread and common than is realised. Numbers of people gave me examples that they mistakenly thought have lost currency. A middle-aged man remarked that the expressions 'to fall pregnant' or its common abbreviation 'to fall' are not current now, but he is wrong. What has happened is that as a youth he moved away from his close-knit country family, made city friends and contacts who would be unlikely to use these terms, and married a woman from a migrant family whose first language is not English. And so, nowadays, no women he is likely to meet will speak of 'falling' [pregnant].

Much is heard now about the kinds of personal qualities necessary for the formation of good relationships at work, among friends, in marriage and the family. Language is one of the areas where adjustment and give and take are necessary. Les Murray says his wife

says 'pan' where I say 'saucepan'. What I call a 'pan' she calls a 'frying pan'. I guess a similar case is that of hoe: where I tend to say 'hoe', Dad and most older Murrays up the bush say 'chipping hoe' (pronounced by all of us as chippenhoe). They then go on to use 'hoe' for what I'd call a 'mattock'. Though they also say 'mattock' half the time too — and we all pronounce it maddick.

At some stage of his youth Les left the farm and the close company of his father and uncles, and thereafter spoke and/or worked with people whose terms for 'hoe' were new to him. For one reason or another, he adopted the novel and discarded the accustomed. My father, who was born in Auckland, New Zealand and usually retained the names for tools and implements that he learned as a boy, spoke of hoes and mattocks as follows:

The hoe: a Dutch hoe (weeds are scraped by pushing forwards).
Hoe: either a chipping hoe (heavier blade, downward chopping or scraping) or a weeding hoe, a narrow, sharply curved blade with a point (pulled sideways and manoeuvred round the base of plants), or also a weeding hoe has one chisel-shaped blade and one shaped into two hooks.

159

Mattock: virtually the same as a pick but each of its blades was chisel-shaped, one being wider than the other. Heavier in weight than a hoe. *Pick:* I cannot better the *Concise Oxford Dictionary*'s definition. 'Tool consisting of iron bar usually curved with point at one end and point or chisel-edge at other, with wooden handle passing through middle perpendicularly, used for breaking up hard ground etc.

And, for the record, a 'cultivator' was a kind of hoe with three curved and pointed prongs — these were attached with screws and bolts so that its area and kind of use could be regulated.

Domestic confusion often centres around imprecise terminology. 'You'll find tea in the canister labelled "Coffee"; sugar's in "Flour", flour's in the big bin on the floor labelled "Bread". I keep bread in the freezer.'

'What do you use for a wooden spoon?'

'Either that plastic doohickey or the flexible spatula.'

Les Murray was born at Bunyah on the lower north coast of New South Wales, a farming and timber-getting district settled from the Manning around 1870 by Murrays who were mostly of the first Australian-born generation of their Scottish family. He gave me a list of Bunyah usages which is interesting for its region but also because so much of it is universal in Australian speech.

Old: mostly a pejorative 'up home'; when applied to things, it connotes shabbiness, wear and inferiority as compared with 'new', bright, modern things. *Old* rarely carried prestige at home; many people there haven't even now fully caught up with the city vogue for antiques and bygones and will cheerfully prefer modern laminex furniture to fine old oak, though they will be wary of selling the old furniture cheaply. Few of them were ever taken in that easily, when the city-ites came prospecting some years ago. My father was once roundly scolded by a house-

160

keeper from the city who came to work for us believing that when dad advertised that he had an 'old' house, he didn't mean a shabby, decrepit one, but a solid, old-world comfortable one. *Bought:* versus *homemade.* In everything except cakes, the shop product outranked the homemade or homegrown one up home, and this is only gradually changing now. My father still used 'good as a bought one' as a term of approval. Even for parts of the body when they've recovered from injury!

(In these days when governments regulate advertising and insist on certain ethical standards the sign 'Home-made Cakes' is an interesting survival from less honest eras. When I was a child a tremendous treat was a bought cake from a shop called Isobels, or a Sargent's cake in town. And the whole point of the treat was that the shop cake was more elaborate, or richer, or more thickly iced than cakes from the home oven. It puzzled me then that these shops advertised 'Home Made Cakes', and it does now. A 'Continental Cake Shop' nowadays seems to mean one selling what Australians call Danish pastry and a few fruit flans. A shop calling itself a 'Patisserie' is sometimes, not always, a safer bet. N.K.)

Herrin' gutted: pronounced *hair*in' gutted, the long vowel indicating Scottish origins — a curious pejorative still occasionally heard. Comparable with 'stallion-eyed' meaning crazily staring, probably mad. I once heard a man cop the following full blast: 'You miserable herrin' gutted stallion-eyed shiverin' shakin' whore's bastard!' (I have included these terms for interest although they are not, I think, used in Familyspeak. N.K.)

Miserable: in the sense of mean, stingy rather than sad. A miserable, too-exacting shopkeeper is sometimes called near: 'He's too near for my liking'.

Useless: bush and working people's pejorative, meaning everything from lazy or clumsy through to helpless or crippled. Harsh attitudes underlie this word. In expansive moods a useless bastard might be described ironically as an 'ornament' or 'decoration', usually as compared with the speaker, who might call him or herself a 'working model'.

Forsaken: short for God-forsaken: this, too, is often used of per-

161

sons, as a pejorative, and given the usual elision of -ing to -en, a lot of people use it as if the word were God-forsaking, i.e that the person, rather than the deity, had done the forsaking! I like the instinctive piety here, which gets God off the hook. (I am particularly grateful to Murray for reminding me of this word because it is widely heard and probably venerable, but not collected by Baker, Wilkes or Hornadge. God-forsaken has affinities with God-forgotten, celebrated by Peter Airey at the turn of the century.* N.K.)

> Lies the town of God-forgotten duly west,
> Sleep the folks in God-forgotten like the blest,
> And the dreary plains that bound it
> Sweep their drowsy blast around it
> Till you nod and drawl, "Confound it! Let us liquor — let us rest!"

> And it blinks, does God-forgotten, through the blaze,
> And it winks, does God-forgotten, through the haze
> And its eyes are mostly bleary,
> And its voice is mostly beery
> And its intellect is dozing in a chronic state of daze ...

Where: 'I read where they can cure arthritis nowadays.' Also, 'He only told them that where they'd leave him alone.'
Condition: fat, on humans or animals. 'Geez, Les, you've put on condition lately.' The opposite is 'poor': 'Them heifers are looking as poor as wood/piss/Job's turkeys.'
Poor: also used as a title of the dead. 'That was the year poor Tom got bit with the snake.'
Cordial: any soft drink, aerated or not, though syrups to which water was added were often called 'Mynor' or 'fifty-fifty' [50-50] after popular proprietary brand names. (Cordial in this sense is fairly widespread in Australia and seems to perpetuate an outmoded English standard usage.)

Australian Bush Ballads, D. Stewart and N. Keesing; Angus & Robertson, 1956.

Dry Bible: a condition of cattle in which one or more of their stomachs becomes immovably jammed with food. Can be fatal. By extension, something utterly exasperating can cause the exclamation 'Wouldn't it give you the dry bloody Bible!'

Falling away: in the sense of losing weight. 'By Hell young Fred has fell away — he's as poor as a kangaroo dog lately.' Speaking of falling away and the foods which help you do so, have you ever heard of 'bread and scratch?' or 'honeymoon salad' (lettuce alone)?

Gulling, horsing: on heat. Also means being exasperatingly foolish: 'Garn, yer horsing!' A horse, pronounced in a special, emphatic way, is an old euphemism for a stallion; cf. 'stone horse' or 'entire horse'. (Australians also use 'horsing' in the sense of 'playing the fool'/indulging in 'horse play'. Americans use 'horsing' in that sense, too N.K.)

Springing: pregnant; usually, but not exclusively, applied to animals.

Easy as pee-the-bed-awake: very easy indeed. A boringly intricate job, on the other hand, is said to be like 'picking fly dirt from pepper'.

Green cart: vehicle allegedly sent to convey mad people to the asylum. 'He wants to look out, they'll be sending the green cart for him next.' Pronounced almost as one word, *green*cart. (This is akin to a threat of my city childhood, 'the black Maria' will get you. In the 1920s and 30s police lock-up vans were cumbersome black vehicles. Nowadays the vans are blue and usually called 'paddy-wagons'.* One other strange vehicle hails from Mount Morgan, Queensland. 'The bodysnatcher' was the mine motor vehicle that, in the event of an emergency or breakdown late at night or early morning, was sent to fetch a needed tradesman; he had to be woken and get dressed. The bodysnatcher pre-dated widespread domestic telephones and car ownership. N.K.)

Dinner: lunch, in town person's parlance.

Tea: dinner.

Supper: dinner.

Cup of tea: a minor meal or snack.

Cup-of-tea dinner: a light, uncooked lunch.

Evening: includes afternoon, as morning includes forenoon even in urban speech. The evening milking started around four o'clock in the afternoon, or earlier.

Throw a seven: ropeable, frothing at the mouth. This is an old expression for throwing a pink fit, having a tantrum of major proportions. People 'up home' never spoke of getting angry, but rather of getting wild. Getting just a bit wild was called getting 'scotty'. This tended to be said to children: 'Be good now. I'm a bit scotty with you.' To show that anger wasn't exclusively Scots, though, we also spoke, and still speak of having a terrible 'Paddy', or getting our 'Paddy out' (or up). There are lots of these old Paddy expressions, often denigratory of the Irish: 'Paddy's lantern' (the moon). To be rankling over something, to be annoyed at someone, is often described as 'having your arse in your hand': 'He's got his arse in his hand with you properly.' (Baker notes that 'to throw a seven' derives from dicing. In World War II slang the term, which carries connotations of bad luck, meant to die. N.K.)

---

*See *Throw a seven.*

Old Year's Night: although of Scots extraction, we never say *Hogmanay* for the eve of New Year's Day. Being Scots, the old settlers 'up home' made more of this than they did of Christmas, holding large and increasingly noisy parties that led up to the singing 'of Auld Lang Syne'; a real 'shivoo'. That bush word for a large party, especially a house party, is said to come from the French *chez vous* (at your place). ('Shivoo' is long-lived and widespread in town and country in Australia. N.K.)

Fightable: extremely angry, ready to fight: 'The old man was wild about that hole in his fence — he was fightable over it, when he first found it.'

Fight a woman: expression of ironically idiotic over-confidence in one's fitness: 'By damn! I'm so healthy I could fight a woman!'

Feed: a meal: 'We had a good feed at the Greeks.' Also a meal of some particular food temporarily available or in season: 'There's about five feeds of beans left in the garden.' This expression dates from the days before fridges or the 'icechest', the corned meat era.

Candlebark: rotted outer layer of dead timber, used as kindling for fires and fuel stoves.

Bandicooting: digging potatoes, onions or other root vegetables with your bare hands, often in the course of theft.

Port: in the sense of a suitcase, this is a predominantly Queensland usage that is heard as far down the coast as Bunyah and clear down to Newcastle.

Muttai or *mutteye:* green or unparched corn suitable for boiling and eating with butter as corn-on-the-cob. The word is cited in Tucker's *Ralph Rashleigh,* and is almost certainly an early Aboriginal borrowing.

Worst in the world: notoriety, public opprobrium, a disgrace. 'Old Mother Mag saw me riding home drunk last week, so I s'pose I'll be the worst in the world now.'

Neither me arse nor me elbow: something indefinite or indifferent, a person who lacks decision or distinctiveness.

Book: any bound item of printed matter. Referring to things by their roughest, most poverty-stricken names — 'rag' for 'cloth', 'boot' for 'shoe', or 'shack' for 'house' — and refusing to distinguish between a book and a magazine, was a way of parading cultural deprivation, real or assumed, and of crying poormouth. It was a defiance of townie cultivation and, ultimately, of fate.

(This Bunyah usage does not, explain the widespread use of 'book' for 'magazine'. It is an Australian mis-usage that bedevils the local book trade and even makes for difficulties in preparing simple questionnaires for market research. It is one of the rare instances in speech where educational differences are apparent; the other is the pronunciation of the letter 'H'. Products of the Roman Catholic education system frequently say 'haitch' — nearly all other speakers say 'aitch'. To refer to the *Women's Weekly* as a book is incorrect speech. N.K.)

Budget: old ladies, when I was a child, still often used this word to mean a magazine. More up-to-date people said journal.

Good House: most modern part of a farmhouse; a family grown more affluent might build a modern house or at least a few rooms with 'modern' ceilings and wall lining alongside the earlier unlined slab house and join the two by means of a walkway. It was then a matter of conservatism, habit, 'flashness' and family needs which house they tended to prefer to be in. The 'good room' was the parlour, entered only on ceremonial occasions. And other 'good' things rarely used because they were too good to use included Sunday tablecloths, Sunday crockery and good crystalware.

Duckback: mythical basis of all foods that come to the table while still too hot. 'What sort of soup is this, Dad?' 'It's duckback soup, son: mind you don't burn your mouth.' From the action of ducking or flinching back from something hot.

Squawmish: pronounced *squor*mish: nauseous, sick in the stomach. 'When I saw the maggots I got all squawmish in the belly.' I am pretty sure this word is Border Scots, brought to Australia by the Murrays. It is used by folk of Dad's generation, but not so much now. Comparable with 'squeamish'. (Both the word and the pronunciation are widespread, at least in NSW. N.K.)

*Googery:** a small roofed shed, open on one side, in which a fire was lit to boil water, heat branding irons, etc. Very occasionally a googery had a gesture in the direction of a chimney, but

166

mostly there was just a flat or sloping roof of bark or iron. *Washhouse:* when a farmhouse acquired a modern kitchen with an iron stove the former detached kitchen or 'cookhouse'* with its open fire and chains for slinging iron pots was often relegated to the status of an outside laundry.

Cowtime: milking time. All life, and I mean *all* life, on small farms was conducted 'between milkings'. Great virtue inhered in one's readiness to get up before dawn and 'sneak up on the cows in the dark' as my father put it, so as to have the morning milking done by sunrise. Afternoon milking started around 3.30-4.30 p.m. Milking after dark was a disgrace, unless the cause was serious, such as an illness in the family. Lives were delimited by the distance people could travel from home between milkings, and many a youth enlisted, in both wars, to escape the tyranny of Rosie and old Bessie! Milking was often called 'stripping Strawberry', and it was done at 'the bails' or the 'dairy-and-bails' (the dairy was originally a separate building with a copy of the Pure Food Act of 1908 pinned to the compulsorily whitewashed wall). Terms like 'cowshed' were wholly foreign. While awaiting milking, the cows stood together in the 'yard' or 'cowyard' and when milked they were turned out into the 'night paddock', the 'day paddock' or whatever. They might sometimes be put into 'the cultivation' to graze on weeds, cornstalks and the like; any field set aside for crops was called 'the cultivation', and one spoke of 'ploughing up a paddock for cultivation'. A farm, especially a dairy farm, was also called a 'place': 'Her father's going to leave her a 300-acre place when he dies'. The rope which restrained a fractious cow from running backwards out of her bail was called a 'britchin' (from breeching, I

---

*Les and I speculated whether 'googery' might have derived, via googy egg, from a family name for a hen-house or laying-shed, but he now thinks that a likelier derivation is that the first two buildings the old settlers invariably used to put up were a tent to sleep in and a shed or shelter to keep the rain off their fire. They called this shelter the 'cookhouse', and Les remembered, from very early childhood, that this was his other name for the googery, too! From 'cookhouse' to 'googery' seems a simple progression: cookhouse — cookery — googery.

presume), and her tendencies to kicking were forestalled, often, with a 'legrope' on her nearside ankle. Nowadays, but not in my time, milkers — the cows, not the people! — are dehorned usually and have their tails docked, so that the delights of a dungladen tail swishing accurately across one's open eyes are almost a bygone affair. While milking, we did not usually sit on a stool, but on a 'block', a section of hardwood tree-trunk polished to a high shine at the top or sitting end by years of firm contact with buttocks wrapped in sturdy cloth. After milking machines (the machines) came along, we usually only sat on the block to 'start' a cow or to 'strip' her, i.e. get the last of her milk after taking off the 'teatcups'. Cows not 'in milk' were 'dry', usually because they were 'in calf' (pregnant). Old cows pretty much beyond their usefulness (though cows don't have a menopause and so can breed till they die) are called 'crackers'. A calf is also known as a 'poddy', and if male and allowed to grow up so, it is called successively a 'bull calf', a 'bull' and, if castrated in adulthood, a 'stag', or else it is successively a 'bull calf', a 'steer'

and a 'bullock'; if female, it is a 'heifer calf', a 'heifer' ('joined' or 'unjoined'), a 'cow' and a 'cracker'.
A cow is also the answer to the riddle
What is it that has

two hookers
two lookers
four standers
four dilly-danders
and a swishabout?

Pardon me for spelling out what may be familiar terms — not all city folk know them. They are not wholly domestic terms but were and are as well known to country women and children as to country men, since everyone shares the work on a small farm.

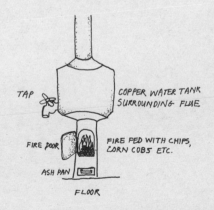

MOORHOUSE BOILER: A columnar water heater, invented by Frank Moorhouse's father, found on most dairy farms.

15

We're
a weird (looking) mob

YOU LOOK LIKE A DEAD DUCK IN A THUNDERSTORM

Graveyard chompers

A face like a festered pickle bottle

Chucking a bridge

HE'S LOWER THAN A SNAKE'S BELLY

He wouldn't know a tram was up him
till it rang its bell and the people
started getting out

In an earlier vanished Sydney of brown sandstone and brick buildings low to the skyline, a strapping young fellow might be described as large and strong enough 'to pull a bullock wagon up Druitt Street'. The phrase is remembered but no longer used. 'How long would it be since bullock carts laboured up that hill?' wrote the man who contributed it.

'And how long,' I wondered, 'since Australians coined such a complimentary expression?' We seem chary of praising anyone for prowess or appearance except in the most back-handed fashion. 'Mary is quite a nice little cook' we say patronisingly even if Mary weighs in at 95 kilograms and is 'two pick handles wide across the bottom', or 'Bob isn't a bad sort of carpenter'. One woman wrote that her mother (born 1886) and grandmother intended fond approval when they described her 'black-lashed eyes, surrounded by light brown pigmentation of the eyelid area … as having been put in with a smutty finger'.

Much of our colloquial speech suggests that we are not only 'a weird mob'* but sour and grudging, too.

---

*They're a Weird Mob, John O'Grady (Nino Culotta), Ure Smith, 1957

In the 1920s a young housewife walked out of her house for a rare day in town. As her daughter recalls, she worked hard, long hours as a rule, having 'no mod cons, a large family and *there really wasn't much opportunity for jaunting for pleasure*'. (My italics, N.K.) The young woman wore her rarely used gloves and carried a handbag, which she probably called her 'purse'. She had not walked far along the roadway when an elderly neighbour spotted her, looked her up and down sourly, and said, 'Hmm. It's well to be *you!*'

Presumably, since she later told the story against herself and her daughter still recalls it, that young woman refused to allow 'a pack of old tabbies' to spoil her rare day out. If they followed her with envious eyes and gossiped about her with malicious tongues, saying she was 'dressed to kill' or 'dressed up to the nines' or that she fancied herself as 'the cat's meouw', perhaps she comforted herself by reflecting that her wrinkled persecutors had faces 'like road maps' or 'run over jam tins' or 'the back ends of tram smashes', 'ham fisted' to an old chook and ugly as 'a hatful of monkeys' while they mouthed their nastiness through 'graveyard chompers' (false teeth).

In 'our book' the major sin is not in saying something wounding and cutting, but in saying it behind our victim's back. Domestically we seem to carry this notion of virtue to almost unbelievable heights, or depths, of unkindness. If we think one of our loved ones looks 'like death warmed up' or 'a dead duck in a thunderstorm' or 'an accident getting ready to happen'; if their morning-after eyes remind us of 'two piss holes in the snow' we do not hesitate to tell them so and, what is more, we expect our victims to accept our honest, outspoken remarks with good grace. Anyone who resents home truths and shows it with a face 'like a bagful of sour lemons' is a rotten sport and 'as ugly as sin, too'.

In even the most idealistic households, however, insult occasionally goes 'beyond a joke' and leads to blows when the protagonists tend to end up with faces that look as if 'they've been chasing parked cars'.

Despite Australia's multi-cultural and, in many areas, multilingual society we continue to cherish, against all odds and visual evidence, a national stereotype of ourselves as lean, vigorous, tanned and tall, with hatchet jaws and saturnine expressions despite recent medical and dietary research suggesting that significant numbers are overweight if not positively obese: 'beef to the ankles'.

For every podgy child who reminds its fond relatives of 'a baby elephant', 'tub of lard' or 'pumpkin head', there is one who is 'as skinny as a walking hairpin', or 'a yard of pump water', or 'a gas pipe cut on the bias', or 'a shaved match-stick', or 'a thread of cotton'.

'If she turned side-on you'd never see her, and she'd slip through a crack in the floorboards.'

A very tall person is 'not long on weight'. A bandy person — 'he'd never stop a pig in a poke' — walks 'as if he has a grass seed between his legs' (or elsewhere). 'Old dot and carry one' walks with a limp; 'paddle feet' walks clumsily.

'Here comes Miss Gawky with her knees hitting her jaw!'

Children who grimace or 'pull faces' are warned that if the clock should stop or the wind change while they are contorting their features, they will look like *that* lifelong.

'pumpkin head'

A person with buck teeth sports 'a good pair of corned-beef grabbers' with which she 'could eat an apple through a paling fence' or 'a slice of watermelon through wire-netting'.

Protruding ears resemble 'a head like a wing nut' or 'a Morris Minor [car] with the doors open'.

'Zits' or 'ackers' (pimples) may be 'subterraneous' or 'volcanos', and acne sufferers have faces 'like a festered pickle bottle', or a 'lumpy rice pudding'. It is usually faces far older than those plagued by acne that resemble 'a kind cow', 'a bar-room floor' or 'a road accident'.

Faces can also be 'so hard they must have been fed on rock cakes'. As we are wont to exclaim, 'I've seen better heads on a glass of beer.' Of bald heads it may be said that 'grass doesn't grow on a busy track'. As for men who sport long or thick beards, 'it's a mean dog that barks from behind a hedge'.

'I'd like to have that nose full of gold-dust/halfpennies' explains itself. A girl who 'chucks a bridge' sits with her underpants visible.

While many of these expressions apply to either sex a few phrases that could be interchangeable seem only to apply to men. These sometimes acquire a note of bitterness when they are uttered by women, and particularly when they are used by badly treated women referring to irresponsible, violent or, conversely, pusillanimous men. Because of this sort of resonance some phrases that occur in general slang have a place of their own in Sheilaspeak, too. Among these are: 'He's so crooked he couldn't lie straight in bed'; 'He's lower than a snake's belly (or a lizard drinking)'; 'He's so low he has to reach *up* to touch bottom'; 'He's so tight you'd have to hammer a pin up his bum with a sledgehammer'; and 'He wouldn't know a tram was up him till it rang its bell and the people started getting off'. A despicable man may be too stupid, or too cowardly, 'to find/fight his way out of a paper bag'.

One South Australian correspondent made the very good point that women do not use sexual innuendo in the way men do:

Teenagers may giggle every time the words 'period' or 'thing' come up, but life, death and birth become deadly earnest for older women.

I have often talked with a group of men and realised to my horror they were (teasingly) taking everything I said the wrong way. The simplest example is that 'hot' has to be sexual and not to do with the weather, likewise 'green' is not a colour. Almost any phrase can be given sexual connotations by emphasis — 'So he wants you to *work* for him.' I have found this all the way from uneducated working class to professor. It is all part of the battle of the sexes.

What woman would say '*the* wife'? It's '*my* husband'.

Likewise the Australian male alone says 'Just as well the cook's here', meaning wife and mother.

Our children's books always referred to 'the lady' or 'girl' but in real life she was 'the woman' 'cow' 'old sow' 'old wether' 'bitch' — more derogatory if preceded by 'old'.

16

Shut your mouth, there's a bus coming!

TALKING THE LEG OFF AN IRON POT

Bible bashers

She chucked a willy

Save your breath to cool your porridge

UP THE CREEK WITHOUT A PADDLE

'I ought to hang you on the wall
for a picture.'

'Your language was not only obscene, but disgusting, particularly when it was used in the presence of a police officer,' Mr E. N. Loane, SM told a man who had pleaded guilty in the Rockhampton Magistrate's Court yesterday to an obscene language charge.

Morning Bulletin, Rockhampton, 3 September 1981

Had the offender spoken his foul remarks in front of mere civilians or 'littlies' would his words have been a lesser atrocity and been punished more lightly than the $75 fine, in default of one month's imprisonment, that the magistrates dished out to him? (He was an unemployed youth aged seventeen.)

Fortunately, I feel reasonably confident that any Queensland 'fuzz' into whose trembling hands this book may fall will be safe from corruption or affront to his fragile sensibilities. Although abundant profanity and some exceedingly coarse remarks are a noticeable feature of Australian general slang, positive obscenity is absent from Familyspeak despite its loquacious nature and frequent pre-occupation with the kind of person who 'could talk under twenty feet of wet cement ... (pause) ... with a mouthful of toffee'.

This is not to say that the argot of abuse is unknown to juvenile and domestic Australia, but it tends to be of the order of, 'Arr, yer think yer a flowerpot 'cos yer got a hole in yer bottom!' Occasionally, it is less innocuous, but not on the score of gross indecency.

One such example is curious because it derives from that

181

most saccharine of indigenous characters, Skippy the Kangaroo. As is well known and widely deplored, Australian general slang employs a battery of racist phrases such as 'wog', 'bog', 'Itie' and 'chow'. Some people who 'do their marbles' use these terms with deliberate and trouble-making intent. In Sydney and Melbourne, groups of Greek youths, understandably sick and tired of being taunted as 'wogs' by counterparts of Anglo-Saxon appearance, have taken to retaliating with 'skips!' or 'skippies!'. In some quarters this usage has become a rallying call to battles that have resulted in bloodshed, bruises and court appearances. If and when knives have been produced retribution has been severe, but otherwise southern magistrates and police have been understanding and have let both factions off lightly with warnings, lectures from the Bench, and bonds.

The irritation caused by the kind of person who 'could talk the leg off an iron pot', may be unintentional but none the less infuriating. A woman exasperated her work-mates with never-ending chatter until one of them exclaimed, 'Your perpetual motion gives me corns in the ears!' Thereafter, her nickname was Perpetual Motion.

A woman of that stamp will talk 'till the cows come home' or 'till the cow calves or cracks its neck'. 'If her mouth was a bridge you'd never cross it.' According to many correspondents they are often described as 'blatherskites'.*

Some of us talk very rapidly 'like machine guns', others drawl 'as if their words got lost along the way'. Some sound as if 'they have a plum in their mouths' while those who gesticulate excessively 'couldn't talk if they lost their arms' (or 'were hand-

---

* This term is reported to be most often used by Australians of Irish descent. S. J. Baker, *The Australian Language* (p. 138), says the Scottish 'bletherskite' became 'blatherskite' in America and 'bladderskite' in Australia but in numerous reports to me the spelling, or pronunciation, was always 'blatherskite'.

cuffed'). An English father (born circa 1853) who complained that his daughter sounded 'like a trumpet lined with tripe', however, was merely commenting on her lack of singing ability.

Door-to-door salesmen, market researchers and 'God-botherers' who call uninvited, get a toe inside people's doors and then 'talk them blind' are an intolerable nuisance to many families, and particularly to elderly or over-polite people who feel unable to ask them to leave. My father perfected a formula for dealing with 'Bible bangers' (or 'Bible bashers') which I use with success: 'I am *so* glad you have a religion that consoles and satisfies you. I have, too, I am happy to say.' Then shut the door.

183

My mother's pet hate was 'organ recitals' given by the sort of person who, when you ask politely 'How are you?' tells you at length and in detail. Some people who utter strings of complaints have perhaps found that 'the wheel that makes the most noise gets the oil'. The woman who talks on and on and on about nothing in particular resembles 'a squeaky gate in a breeze'. An outspoken, or sometimes an impertinent speaker, 'has too much of what the cat licks itself with'. (Too much tongue.)

A Queensland woman born at the turn of the century perpetuates a fine phrase for those occasions when, in the middle of a story, one's mind goes a complete blank. 'I was shooting and the [gun] powder got wet.' Someone who has been woolgathering during a general conversation, or who has missed hearing some important point, may be taunted with the hoary riddle: 'Where was Moses when the light went out? Under the bed looking for matches.'

People whose blabbermouths resemble 'torn pockets' are somewhat like the proverbial boy who too often cried, 'Wolf!' After a while no one pays any attention to their words. But when normally quietly spoken and calm persons suffer extreme provocation or are indignant to an unusual degree and really 'let fly', their hearers are more likely to sit up and take notice. After the outburst has subsided those family members who may have prompted an uncharacteristic protest will long remember the day mum 'blew her top', 'snapped her twig', 'popped her cork', 'hit the roof', 'did her block' and 'chucked a willy'.

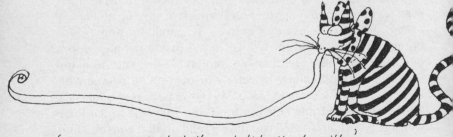

'too much of what the cat licks itself with'

Speech resembles other areas of human life and endeavour: it is much more effective to keep your powder dry until 'the psychological moment' presents itself. She who forgets this, and 'goes off half-cocked' deserves the scorn of 'keep your shirt on', or 'don't panic' or 'don't get off your bike, I'll pick up your pump', or 'save your breath to cool your porridge'.

Superficially, a good deal of Familyspeak sounds abusive, unkind, earthy and occasionally, bawdy. Within its range, however, a recognisable censorship operates by folk consensus. This first became plain to me during a radio talk-back session. In the course of these conversational give and takes, categories quickly became established as one caller reminds those waiting their turn of items they use themselves. On this occasion several successive women instanced well-known general slang terms for drunkenness: 'High as a kite', 'full as a boot', 'blithered' and so on. When I suggested 'full as a goog' as an additional term the phone-callers disagreed strongly, and several women followed up the discussion in letters. 'Full as a goog'* and also 'full as a tick', they said, *always and only* refer to being full of food — well fed after a meal — and are synonymous with 'full up to dolly's wax' (or pussy's bow). There was less unanimity, however, about 'full as a family jerry' (or po). In some families this refers only to insobriety, in others always to being well fed, but some families use it in either sense.

An elderly correspondent whose family's traditional colloquialisms reached, through parents and grandparents, into Sydney's distant past (circa 1830s and perhaps earlier), wrote that 'tight as a mouse's ear' generally denoted a stingy man but had a quite different meaning when it was said of a woman. The context of the letter suggested a vulgar sexual connotation and distinguished the expression in this sense from general family speech.

Familyspeak contains numerous phrases that have different meanings in a domestic setting from when they are used more

---

*This is plainly not so as far as general/male slang is concerned, see p. 140.

coarsely among adults, or in predominantly male gatherings. Two examples are 'in and out like a fiddler's elbow' or 'rushing around like a one-armed fiddler with the itch' whose innocuous meanings merely describe useless or senseless over-activity.

Some letter-writers and other informants took a great deal of trouble to list colloquial examples in categories, and a few of these further divided their examples to include a section they consider 'rude' or 'a bit vulgar'. From this sort of evidence I conclude that certain phrases seem 'rude' to one informant, but not to another; some of these merely reflect differing degrees of tolerance for less than polite words and phrases — one woman's bum is another woman's 'behind' or 'sit upon'. An occasional usage listed as 'rude' seemed so harmless that, for the life of me, I can't discover a hidden or double meaning. But other expressions very obviously mean either different things to different speakers, or are used in very different ways according to circumstances and present company. An example is 'to be left up the creek without a paddle' which is sometimes used to describe a person of either sex or any age who is in a dilemma: 'Millie said she'd pick the kids up in her car after sport, but she had a flat [tyre] and they were left up the creek without a paddle.' But in general slang, and very frequently in Sheilaspeak, this phrase (sometimes given as 'up shit creek') more specifically describes an unmarried girl who has fallen pregnant.

Individual family ideas of suitability and good taste also operate. In phrases like 'scarce as rocking-horse [excreta]' some people say 'shit' and others use 'dirt'.

An example of how some colloquialisms become family jokes is the father who used to tease his wife by exclaiming, 'It's so cold it would freeze the balls off ... (long pause) ... a billiard table!' Presumably, after a few cold mornings mother was not really on tenterhooks but his practised accomplice in the act; and after a while his expectant, giggling children also understood the precise point of the joke in which everyone acted their given role.

Words and phrases that are widespread in Familyspeak are never frightening or threatening. If a word or phrase cannot be

186

used or explained lovingly, and in terms that children can comprehend and find graphic or funny, then those usages are rejected. 'I ought to hang you on the wall for a picture' or 'If you do that again I'll murder you as sure as God made little apples' are perceived as exasperated, but harmless, threats. A metaphor like 'cold as a stepmother's breast', however, though relatively common in the community, does not seem to be used domestically, presumably because its explanation might be hurtful and even menacing to young children.

Despite the conservative traditionalism of Familyspeak, over time it reflects alterations to community tolerance and acceptance of certain words and attitudes, but these changes enter domestic language more slowly than general slang. As I also said earlier,* it seems that many women who avoid any kind of impolite speech away from home, experience amusement and relief by relaxing their standards of gentility within their own four walls and when speaking to young children or using Sheilaspeak among women friends.

Standards of propriety across generations differ widely, especially as to functions of the body. One woman of eighty-five was apologetic about sending me a phrase containing the word 'widdle', because, as she wrote, everyone nowadays speaks of 'going to the toilet' and the everyday expressions of her youth are regarded, she thinks, as rude by younger people. Older generations of women frequently avoided the words 'constipate' and 'constipation' which were thought to be crude and, perhaps by some women, lewd. Indeed in some groups and areas these words were taboo. Euphemisms like 'bound-up' were used and, conversely, 'binding medicine' was given for diaorrhea, while 'loosening' medicine was sometimes preferred to 'laxative'.

Many people still disapprove of the widespread issuance of 'damn' and 'bloody' from the lips of children whose young adult parents scarcely notice. Certain words remain taboo; for the moment 'fuck' and 'cunt' seem to be absent from domestic speech but they are entering Sheilaspeak; sooner or later they

---

*See Chapter 2.

will infiltrate Familyspeak. But, as with their hitherto avoided predecessors, when that happens it will certainly be because their aggressive connotations and shock value have largely disappeared in the wider community.

'Ta—Ta'

'Cheerio'

'Bye-bye'

'HOORAY'

'Hoo Roo'